The Saber and Scroll Journal

Also from Westphalia Press
westphaliapress.org

The Idea of the Digital University

Dialogue in the Roman-Greco World

The History of Photography

International or Local Ownership?: Security Sector Development in Post-Independent Kosovo

Lankes, His Woodcut Bookplates

Opportunity and Horatio Alger

The Role of Theory in Policy Analysis

The Little Confectioner

Non-Profit Organizations and Disaster

The Idea of Neoliberalism: The Emperor Has Threadbare Contemporary Clothes

Social Satire and the Modern Novel

Ukraine vs. Russia: Revolution, Democracy and War: Selected Articles and Blogs, 2010-2016

James Martineau and Rebuilding Theology

A Strategy for Implementing the Reconciliation Process

Issues in Maritime Cyber Security

A Different Dimension: Reflections on the History of Transpersonal Thought

Iran: Who Is Really In Charge?

Contracting, Logistics, Reverse Logistics: The Project, Program and Portfolio Approach

Unworkable Conservatism: Small Government, Freemarkets, and Impracticality

Springfield: The Novel

Lariats and Lassos

Ongoing Issues in Georgian Policy and Public Administration

Growing Inequality: Bridging Complex Systems, Population Health and Health Disparities

Designing, Adapting, Strategizing in Online Education

Pacific Hurtgen: The American Army in Northern Luzon, 1945

Natural Gas as an Instrument of Russian State Power

New Frontiers in Criminology

Feeding the Global South

Beijing Express: How to Understand New China

The Rise of the Book Plate: An Exemplative of the Art

The Saber and Scroll Journal

Volume 9, Number 4 • Spring 2021

Lew Taylor, editor-in-chief
Jeff Ballard, editor

Westphalia Press
An imprint of Policy Studies Organization

The Saber and Scroll Journal
Volume 9, Number 4 • Spring 2021

All Rights Reserved © 2021 by Policy Studies Organization

Westphalia Press
An imprint of Policy Studies Organization
1527 New Hampshire Ave., NW
Washington, D.C. 20036
info@ipsonet.org

ISBN: 978-1-63723-602-4

Cover and interior design by Jeffrey Barnes
jbarnesbook.design

Daniel Gutierrez-Sandoval, Executive Director
PSO and Westphalia Press

Updated material and comments on this edition
can be found at the Westphalia Press website:
www.westphaliapress.org

TABLE OF CONTENTS

Welcome Letter 1
Chelsea Tatham Zukowski

From Captain America to Watchmen: Comic Book Superheroes
and War in Twentieth Century America 5
Chelsea Tatham Zukowski

The Skagway Commercial Club 21
Jennifer L. Williams

Why the British Lost the American Revolution 41
Gerald Krieger

The Doctrines of Imagination: American Foreign Policy
& the Images of Puerto Rico, 1898-1965 53
Carlos A. Santiago

A Division at War—Part II 67
Dr. Robert Young

The Jewishness of the Babatha Archives 79
Mary Jo Davies

Wild West Shows: An Unlikely Vehicle for the Survival of the
Native American Culture in the Late Nineteenth Century 95
Melissa Sims

Book Review: Brian McAllister Linn's *The Philippine War: 1899–1902* 109
Lewis A. Taylor II

Book Review: Peter Wallenstein's *Blue Laws and Black Codes:
Conflicts, Courts and Change in Twentieth-Century Virginia* 111
Matt Brent

Book Review: Lindsay M. Chervinsky's *The Cabinet: George
Washington and the Creation of an American Institution* 115
Chris Schloemer

Submission Guidelines 119

Welcome Letter

Chelsea Tatham Zukowski

Welcome to the first issue of 2021—a year that brings with it hopes for a brighter, healthier future as we near the finish line of this awful pandemic. More and more people every day are getting vaccinated for COVID-19, and there are growing signs that a sense of "normalcy" is on the horizon. For us here at the *Saber and Scroll Historical Journal*, the events of the past year have instilled an appreciation for the evolution of modern medicine and technology that has allowed us to stay connected, informed, and entertained amid pandemic isolation.

The last year has also brought on many changes—both for us authors and for the journal. This author was pleased to join the editorial team as a contributing editor for the Winter 2020 issue and is honored to have had a hand in bringing this Spring 2021 issue to publication while also having her own work featured. Turn the page for her deep dive into how major comic book superheroes served as political and cultural commentary during war time in twentieth century America.

As for the journal, the editorial staff has decided to publish three issues this year instead of four to ensure we continue to deliver diverse, high quality historical scholarship. This Spring 2021 issue is the first of the year, and will be followed by an issue toward the end of summer/ beginning of fall, and then a third and final issue for winter.

As for this issue, it is a veritable grab bag of historical research and arguments, ranging from the aforementioned survey of American comic books during war to another look at why the British lost the American Revolutionary War. That article presents six ways things went wrong in London at the time that led to a historic loss by the most powerful maritime force in the world.

If you are into late nineteenth century social and culture history like this author, check out the selection on Wild West shows and Native American culture. The article explores how these types of shows were not only some of the most popular forms of entertainment during this time, but how they also gave a safe platform for Native Americans to showcase their customs, traditions, and culture.

If you are looking for a new post-pandemic travel destination, there is a piece about the Skagway Commercial Club's efforts to attract more tourists to the Alaskan city in the early twentieth century. Then there is a look at the evolution of American foreign policy in Puerto Rico from the turn of the century through the mid-twentieth century, including how those policies contributed to opinions about the island's culture and tourism. In another article, early Jewish history takes center stage in a study of the significance of the archive of two-thousand-year-old documents found in a Judaean desert cave in the 1960s.

Rounding out the Spring 2021 issue are three book reviews on various topics including the evolution of the Commonwealth of Virginia's politics, laws, and infrastructure in the twentieth century; how George Washington brought his military expertise to the creation and running of his Cabinet; and a comprehensive look at the "forgotten" Philippine War from 1899 to 1902.

The *Saber and Scroll Historical Journal* team has some specially themed issues coming up later this year encompassing scholarship outside of the United States. The end-of-summer issue will be European history and the Winter issue will have articles focused on world military history. In the meantime, we hope you enjoy this issue and are staying safe and planning for a brighter year ahead.

Ad astra,
Chelsea Tatham Zukowski

Carta de bienvenida

Bienvenidos al primer número de 2021, un año que trae consigo esperanzas de un futuro más brillante y saludable a medida que nos acercamos a la línea de meta de esta terrible pandemia. Cada día más personas se vacunan contra COVID-19, y hay signos crecientes de que hay una sensación de "normalidad" en el horizonte. Para nosotros aquí en Sabre and Scroll Historical Journal, los eventos del año pasado nos han inculcado un aprecio por la evolución de la medicina y la tecnología modernas que nos ha permitido estar conectados, informados y entretenidos en medio del aislamiento pandémico.

El año pasado también ha traído muchos cambios, tanto para nosotros los autores como para la revista. Esta autora se complace en unirse al equipo editorial como editora colaboradora de la edición de invierno de 2020 y se siente honrada de haber participado en la publicación de esta edición de primavera de 2021 y, al mismo tiempo, de presentar su propio trabajo. Pase la página para ver su inmersión profunda en cómo los principales superhéroes de los cómics sirvieron como comentarios políticos y culturales durante la guerra en los Estados Unidos del siglo XX.

En cuanto a la revista, el personal editorial ha decidido publicar tres números este año en lugar de cuatro para garantizar que sigamos brindando estudios históricos diversos y de alta calidad. Este número de primavera de 2021 es el primero del año y será seguido por un número hacia el final del verano / principios del otoño, y luego un tercer y último número para el invierno.

En cuanto a este tema, es una verdadera bolsa de sorpresas de investigación histórica y argumentos, que van desde la encuesta antes mencionada de los cómics estadounidenses durante la guerra hasta otra mirada sobre por qué los británicos perdieron la Guerra Revolucionaria Estadounidense. Ese artículo presenta seis formas en que las cosas salieron mal en Londres en el momento en que provocó una pérdida histórica de la fuerza marítima más poderosa del mundo.

Si te gusta la historia social y cultural de finales del siglo XIX como este autor, echa un vistazo a la selección de espectáculos del salvaje oeste y la cultura nativa americana. El artículo explora cómo este tipo de programas no solo fueron algunas de las formas de entretenimiento más populares durante este tiempo, sino que también brindaron una plataforma segura para que los nativos americanos mostraran sus costumbres, tradiciones y cultura.

Si está buscando un nuevo destino de viaje después de una pandemia, hay un artículo sobre los esfuerzos del Skagway Commercial Club para atraer más turistas a la ciudad de Alaska a principios del siglo XX. Luego hay una mirada a la evolución de la política exterior estadounidense en Puerto Rico desde el cambio de siglo hasta mediados del siglo XX, incluyendo cómo esas políticas contribuyeron a las opiniones sobre la cultura y el turismo de la isla. En otro artículo, la historia judía temprana ocupa un lugar central en un estudio de la importancia del archivo de documentos de dos mil años encontrados en una cueva del desierto de Judea en la década de 1960.

Completan la edición de primavera de 2021 tres reseñas de libros sobre diversos temas, incluida la evolución de la política, las leyes y la infraestructura de la Commonwealth de Virginia en el siglo XX; cómo George Washington aportó su experiencia militar a la creación y funcionamiento de su gabinete; y una mirada completa a la guerra filipina "olvidada" de 1899 a 1902.

El equipo de Sabre and Scroll Historical Journal tiene algunos números especialmente temáticos que surgirán a finales de este año y que abarcan becas fuera de los Estados Unidos. El número de finales de verano será la historia europea y el número de invierno tendrá artículos centrados en la historia militar mundial. Mientras tanto, esperamos que disfrute de este número y se mantenga seguro y esté planeando un año más brillante por delante.

Ad astra,
Chelsea Tatham Zukowski

编者按

欢迎阅读2021年第一期内容。今年的到来伴随着我们对一个更光明、更健康的未来的憧憬，希望尽快结束这场糟糕的大流行。每一天都有越来越多的人获得新冠肺炎（COVID-19）疫苗，并且越来越多的迹象表明，"常态"感就在不久的将来。作为《军刀和卷轴历史期刊》（Saber and Scroll Historical Journal）编辑的我们而言，去年的事件使我们感激现代医药和技术的发展，它让我们在大流行隔离期间能保持联系、知晓信息和娱乐。

去年也对作为作者的我们以及期刊带来了许多挑战。作为2020年冬季期刊的特约编辑，下面这位作者很高兴加入编辑组，并很荣幸能参与出版2021年春季期刊，同时发表她个人的专题文章。请阅读她的深入研究：重要的漫画书超级英雄如何充当20世纪美国战争时期的政治和文化评论者。

至于期刊，编委会成员决定每年发表三期内容，而不是四期，以确保我们持续带来多样化、高质量的历史学术文献。2021年春季期刊是今年的第一期，第二期将于今年夏季末/秋季初出版，第三期将于冬季出版。

至于本期内容，它充满了历史研究和论点的融合，包括上述提及的有关战争时期美国漫画书的调查，和为何英国人在美国革命中战败的研究。后者提出了当时伦敦方面的6个错误，这导致英国作为全世界最强大的海上力量的历史性损失。

如果你像下面这位作者一样喜欢19世纪末的社会历史和文化历史，那么请阅读关于狂野西部秀和本土美国人文化的文章。这篇文章探究了这类表演如何不仅是当时最流行的娱乐形式之一，而且还为本土美国人展示其习俗、传统和文化提供了安全平台。

如果你在寻找大流行后期的新旅游目的地，有一篇关于斯卡圭商业俱乐部的文章值得一读。斯卡圭商业俱乐部在20世纪早期为吸引更多游客来到阿拉斯加而付出了一番努力。下一篇文章研究了20世纪初到20世纪中期美国外交政策在波多黎各的发展，包括这些政策如何促进形成了关于波多黎各文化和旅游业的观点。另一篇文章研究了 20世纪60年代在犹太沙漠（Judaean desert）发现的2000年前留下的资料档案的重要性，重点研究了早期的犹太历史。

2021年春季期刊内容以三篇书评结尾，这三篇书评的主题包括：20世纪弗吉尼亚联邦的政治、法律和基础设施的演变；乔治•华盛顿如何使用其军事才能创建并管理内阁；以及关于1899-1902年间"被遗忘的"菲律宾战争的全面研究。

《军刀和卷轴历史期刊》编辑组在今年还将带来一些特别主题内容，包括来自海外的学术文献。夏季末的发行内容将会是欧洲历史，冬季期刊内容将收录聚焦世界军事历史的文章。同时，我们希望您享受阅读本期内容，注意安全，为更光明的一年做准备。

不断探索（*Ad astra*），

Chelsea Tatham Zukowski

From *Captain America* to *Watchmen*: Comic Book Superheroes and War in Twentieth Century America

Chelsea Tatham Zukowski
American Public University

Abstract

Since their beginnings in the early twentieth century through the post-Cold War era, comic books have entertained readers while also reflecting American cultural ideals amid war and political conflict. Almost every comic book character and superhero ever created in the United States was some sort of reflection of the political or cultural climate in which it was created. It would take volumes to categorize and analyze all the characters' and superheroes' wartime influences, but this survey chronicles the major characters that shaped wartime comic books from World War I through the post-Cold War era following decades of constant conflict. Those characters are Superman, Captain America, Wonder Woman, Iron Man, the Incredible Hulk, Spider-Man, The Dark Knight, and Dr. Manhattan. These characters' stories were not solely about their respective time period's conflict, but their personalities and heroic missions were deeply entrenched in those era's fears, hopes, and cultural ideals. Despite the comic book medium only recently being included and analyzed for its historical scholarship value, this research shows comic books as primary sources for a critical understanding of how American society grappled with war through entertainment.

Keywords: Comic books; superheroes; popular culture; war; the Great War; World War II; Cold War; War on Terror; Captain America; Superman; Iron Man; The Dark Knight; war culture

Del Capitán América a Watchmen: superhéroes del cómic y guerra en los EE. UU. del siglo XX

Resumen

Desde sus inicios a principios del siglo XX hasta la era posterior a la Guerra Fría, los cómics han entretenido a los lectores y al mismo tiempo reflejan los ideales culturales estadounidenses en medio de la guerra y el conflicto político. Casi todos los personajes de cómics y superhéroes creados en los Estados Unidos fueron algún tipo de reflejo del clima político o cultural en el que se crearon. Se necesitarían muchos volúmenes para categorizar y analizar todas las influencias de los personajes y superhéroes en tiempos de guerra, pero esta encuesta relata los personajes principales que dieron forma a los cómics en tiempos de guerra desde la Primera Guerra Mundial hasta la era posterior a la Guerra Fría después de décadas de conflicto constante. Esos personajes son Superman, Capitán América, Wonder Woman, Iron Man, el Increíble Hulk, Spider-Man, The Dark Knight y el Dr. Manhattan. Las historias de estos personajes no trataban únicamente del conflicto de su período de tiempo respectivo, sino que sus personalidades y misiones heroicas estaban profundamente arraigadas en los temores, esperanzas e ideales culturales de esa época. A pesar de que el medio de los cómics se ha incluido y analizado recientemente por su valor académico histórico, esta investigación muestra a los cómics como fuentes primarias para una comprensión crítica de cómo la sociedad estadounidense lidiaba con la guerra a través del entretenimiento.

Palabras clave: Libros de historietas; superhéroes; cultura popular; guerra; la gran Guerra; Segunda Guerra Mundial; Guerra Fría; Guerra en terror; Capitán América; Superhombre; Hombre de Acero; El caballero oscuro; cultura de Guerra

从《美国队长》到《守望者》：二十世纪美国的漫画书超级英雄和战争

摘要

自20世纪早期开始到后冷战时代，漫画书在娱乐读者的同时也反映了战争和政治冲突期间美国的文化理想。美国塑造的几乎每个漫画书角色和超级英雄都在一定程度上反映了当时的政治环境或文化环境。对所有角色和超级英雄的战争时期影响加以分类和分析将花费大量篇幅，但本篇调查按时间顺序记录了从一战到几十年持续冲突之后的后冷战时代期间漫画书的主要角色。这些角色分别为超人、美国队长、神奇女侠、钢铁侠、绿巨人、蜘蛛侠、黑暗骑士和曼哈顿博士。这些角色的故事不仅仅有关于各自时期发生的冲突，他们的个性和英雄使命也根植于当时的恐惧、希望和文化理想。虽然漫画书媒介仅在近年来被用于分析其历史学术价值,但本篇研究表明,漫画书能作为原始资料,用于批判地理解美国社会如何通过娱乐度过战争。

关键词:漫画书,超级英雄,流行文化,战争,一战,二战,冷战,反恐战争,美国队长,超人,钢铁侠,黑暗骑士,战争文

Collins, Marjory, photographer. *New York, N.Y. Children's Colony, a school for refugee children administered by a Viennese. German refugee child, a devotee of Superman.* New York, 1942. October. Photograph. https://www.loc.gov/item/2013649072/.

From the striking political cartoons of World War I and post–Great Depression stories of Superman fighting for the less fortunate, to the violent, anti-heroic sentiments of the Watchmen and the Dark Knight, the comic book medium has housed colorful characters and stories that promoted American ideals and patriotism, criticized political leaders and acts, and reflected feelings and culture during times of war and domestic conflict. In times of war and in times of peace, comic books and their superheroes have been an important piece of America's social fabric since their beginnings in the 1930s as both quirky, colorful entertainment and cultural and historical commentary. Superheroes—namely Superman, Captain America, Batman, and Wonder Woman—are unique cultural icons that have only recently been studied as primary sources and as windows into the history of American culture and entertainment during war times. Just as certain forms of art are products of their times, comic books offer an artistic and entertaining lens through which to study twentieth-century America. Beginning with the first several decades of the 1900s, through World War II, the Cold War era, the post-nuclear era, and the War on Terror, there are many comic book storylines and characters that not only reflect American society during times of foreign and domestic conflict, but they also show how that society reacted. These books are "mythology that is forever adjusting to meet society's needs."[1] Perhaps more than any other medium of entertainment in the twentieth century, superhero comics are primary sources of historical events told through cape-wearing, shield-wielding, superpowered fictional heroes.

DC's Superman is widely considered to be the first comic book superhero in American literature, but before his debut in 1938 and the subsequent superhero boom of World War II, comic strips were primarily devoted to condemning vices like gambling and drinking or supporting a cause in foreign conflicts.[2] Newspapers and periodicals during World War I became famous for publishing short political cartoons that showed the United States as a savior of Europe, condemning Germany and German culture, and promoting American patriotism and the domestic war effort. Though political cartoons are a different medium with a different audience, its use of colorful characters, caricatures, and quote blurbs are a similar style of entertainment and social commentary as that of comic books. It was during World War I that the venerable image of Uncle Sam cemented its place in American literary and art history. Just as "doughboys" became slang for American soldiers and symbolized heroism during the war, Uncle Sam called for patriotic duty in joining the U.S. Army.[3] The poster designed by James Montgomery Flagg was one of 46 the artist did as patriotic propaganda for the U.S. government. The character of Uncle Sam is drawn as a stern, strong older man wearing a blue coat, a red bowtie, and a white hat with a ribbon of white stars on a blue background. The poster reads: "I want YOU for the U.S. Army. Enlist Now."[4] This recruitment poster, done in 1917—when the U.S. entered the war—was a precursor to American comic book artists summing up "an entire national character in the form of a single iconic figure."[5]

For those back home during World War I, comic strips in newspapers and periodicals offered a window into soldiers' lives overseas. Comics like Bud Fisher's "Mutt and Jeff" and Capt. Alban Butler's "Happy Days" allowed "readers of all levels of education to participate virtually in a fight they had to support remotely."[6] Before moving pictures and television, comics were a widely accessible way to promote causes and entertain the masses. Some

"Mutt and Jeff" comic strips promoted buying liberty bonds to support the war effort and had the dynamic duo serve in various Allied armies while poking fun at themselves.[7] Butler, who served in the American First Infantry Division, had his comics contain content "far more meaningful than the simple sight gags might suggest."[8] Butler chronicled his experiences of life in the trenches, foreign food, language barriers, and new cultural customs. While his comics were suitable for younger readers to get an idea of what life as a G.I. was like, his collection also featured underlying moral and political complexities of war.[9]

Charles Schulz' "Peanuts" comics and later animated features memorialized World War I nearly fifty years after it ended. Snoopy, the loveable beagle of the "Peanuts" gang, had his first appearance in 1965 and was drawn pretending his doghouse was a Sopwith Camel biplane. Snoopy became the First World War Flying Ace and "imagined that he flew in hot pursuit of the Red Baron," a title given to German fighter pilot Manfred von Richthofen.[10] Though the "Peanuts" characters and stories didn't appear until decades after the first world war, Carrie Allen Tipton's "Snoopy Remembers the Great War" argues Snoopy's Flying Ace persona and "The Great Pumpkin" animated television special "helped enshrine the memory of the First World War in American popular culture."[11] In the animation, Snoopy dons his pilot outfit and goggles while the children are occupied with their Halloween costumes and plans. Situating himself atop his doghouse, the scene turns into Snoopy imagining himself in a "fierce aerial combat, ending with a crash behind enemy lines, punctuated by staccato artillery."[12] Escaping the crash site, Snoopy then climbs through trenches and passes signs for Châlons-sur-Marne, Pont-à-Mousson, and the River Moselle all while facing the sounds of sirens and machine guns. Schulz and his colleagues later said they did not deliberately aim to commemorate World War I with Snoopy's persona, but the First World War Flying Ace has since become synonymous with Great War and early aviation culture. Four years after his debut, Snoopy as the First World War Flying Ace even accompanied astronauts on the Apollo 10 mission, two months before the first humans landed on the moon.[13]

In the first several decades of the twentieth century, comics acted as illustrated short stories that could be used as propaganda to depict a foreign or domestic enemy to the United States. Before World War II, domestic crime was the main perceived threat to American society depicted in comics. Villainous characters could symbolize corporate greed, labor disputes, or controversial political policies.[14] Though the Great Depression had slowly abated in the late 1930s, the horrors of nationwide economic collapse were still fresh in the American people. Some of the earliest stories of Superman, Batman, and the Green Lantern were of these superheroes taking on corrupt businesses and businessmen who mistreated poor, struggling workers in the 1930s.[15] In his first issues, Superman stopped gangsters from fixing boxing machines, took on smugglers, prevented assassinations,

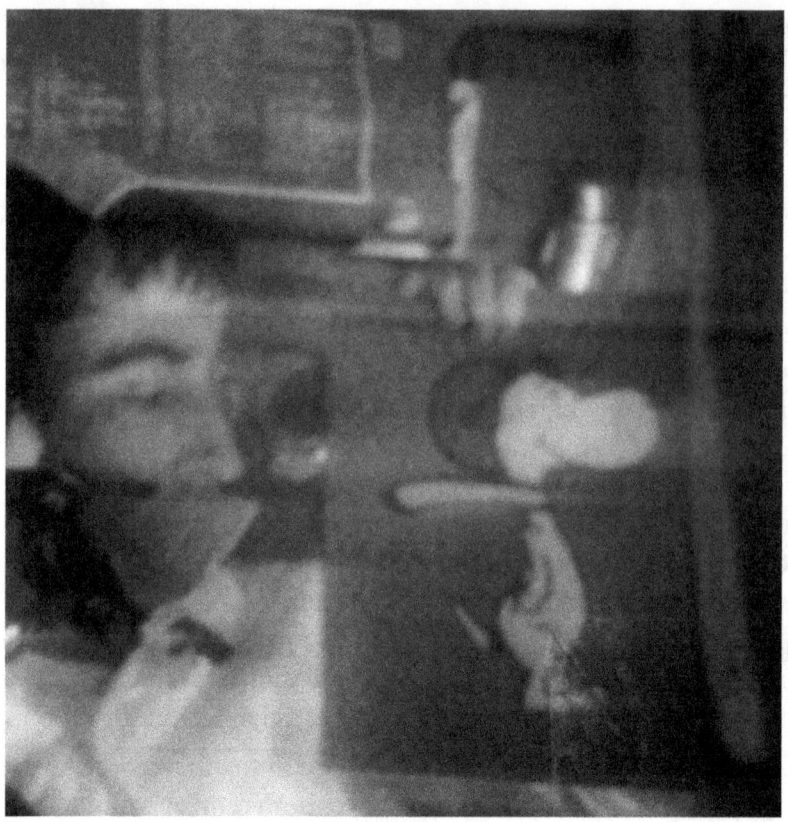

Astronaut John W. Young, Apollo 10 command module pilot, displays a drawing of Snoopy in this color reproduction taken from the fourth telecast made by the color television camera aboard the Apollo 10 spacecraft. When this picture was made the Apollo 10 spacecraft was about halfway to the moon, or approximately 112,000 nautical miles from Earth. Snoopy will be the code name of the Lunar Module (LM) during Apollo 10 operations when the Command Module (CM) and LM are separated. The CM's code name will be Charlie Brown. Also, aboard Apollo 10 were astronauts Thomas P. Stafford, commander; and Eugene A. Cernan, lunar module pilot. Credit: NASA, S69-34076 (19 May 1969)

created decent public housing, and combated political infighting at Metropolis city hall.[16] While Superman at the end of the Great Depression was a social savior, Batman was "an example of the common person helping herself or himself."[17] Though they came from different worlds—literally; Superman is an alien from the planet Krypton—they were both products of the era in which they lived and dealt with enemies and issues as such. These characters and stories made standard the superhero as a defender of the innocent and as socially conscious characters. These original superheroes were "New Deal avengers" who dealt with, discussed, and fought the same social problems plaguing American citizens in the early twentieth century.[18]

By the outbreak of World War II in 1939 and the United States entry into the war in 1941, domestic and foreign conflicts had become as intertwined in comic books as they were in the country.[19] In the 1940s, more than 80 percent of adolescents and more than 90 percent of children were reading comic books.[20] These popular illustrations and stories "helped determine the attitudes of Americans toward issues in the real world, including the use of military force abroad."[21] Leading comic books writers at Marvel Comics and DC discussed and included in their work subtle hints of the need for the United States government to become more involved with issues abroad. Even before the United States entered the war, comics had been attempting to build support among skeptical Americans of the superiority and morality of the Allied cause.[22] Eight months before the Japanese bombed Pearl Harbor, Joe Simon and Jack Kirby published the first issue of "Captain America," a red, white, and blue clad super patriot who fought the enemies of the United States both at home and overseas. While Adolf Hitler proclaimed American popular culture to be inferior to that of any other European country, the first issue of "Captain America" featured a colorful illustration of Captain America punching Hitler in the face.[23]

Simon described Captain America as the "first major comic book hero to take a political stand."[24] During his first appearance in March 1941, Captain America took on sabotage within the U.S. Army, villainous caricatures of German scientists and Nazi leaders attempting to infiltrate the U.S., and the "flaming red terror" of the Red Skull.[25] By the third issue, Marvel Comics co-creator Stan Lee contributed Captain America's first use of his star-spangled shield as a throwing weapon.[26] How the character Steve Rogers came to be Captain America "mimicked the transition the United States needed at the outset of World War II."[27] Steve Rogers was a scrawny weakling unfit for service in the U.S. Army, but a team of government scientists used an experimental serum to transform him into the perfectly strong and moral soldier with superpowers to defend his country. Just as Steve Rogers went from weakling to war machine, the United States transformed from a nation concerned only with itself to a country able to defend itself and crush any enemies.[28]

The American public needed hope and entertainment during World War II, and Captain America's stories provided them, along with the assertion that America's cause and the Allied cause were right and moral. Lee's storylines advocated U.S. intervention and resources, and the Captain America story arcs emphasized Germany's threat to the entire world, explaining the Axis efforts to rule the world through fictional characters and stereotypes.[29] The "Captain America" comics contained all the key elements of contemporary American propaganda: "German atrocities, Allied war goals … vengeance against the evil enemy, and … a sense of adventure and excitement."[30] The stories of Captain America fighting Nazis, the Japanese, and Axis spies helped define the "American way" and asserted

American moral superiority to young readers. Simon and Kirby even gave Captain America a sidekick: 12-year-old Bucky Barnes. With an adolescent sidekick dedicated to the cause and the later foundation of the Sentinels of Liberty youth group, Captain America's comics allowed young readers to "imagine themselves in the action."[31]

Just as the Sentinels of Liberty promoted patriotism in young people on the domestic front, Wonder Woman also promoted the American cause, wore red, white, and blue, and catered to young girls. Though she eschewed traditional gender norms of the time, she rarely took on any of the Axis powers directly. In her early stories, Wonder Woman mostly took on domestic spies, criminals, and "the world's most villainous men."[32] Though the possibility of women in combat was still difficult for readers and the general public to accept, Wonder Woman encouraged children of all ages to collect scrap metal, be vigilant for foreign intervention, and keep faith in the American cause.[33] Comic book superheroes like Wonder Woman and Captain America provided an entertaining escape from a world of violence and death, and acted as an outlet for the young people of America to understand and even take part in a cause that was being promoted as helping America win. Beginning with the comics and characters created during World War II, fighting an enemy during war was not just about physical violence or military tactics—the "common denominator in the struggle against each opponent was patriotism" at home.[34] The American flag became an essential symbol of patriotism during war time. Comic book characters who wear variations of red, white, and blue—including Captain America, Wonder Woman, and the Shield—became "a vehicle for nationalist sentiment."[35]

This pure patriotism and promotion of the United States as "a place where science and equality prevailed over ignorance" continued in comic books long after World War II ended.[36] The Cold War began barely two years after the end of World War II and continued through the end of the 1980s, though it can be explored by the different comic book trends and stories found in the post-war 1950s, the counterculture of the 1960s and the American malaise of the 1970s.[37] While Germany, Nazism, and the Axis powers were the main threats during World War II, the United States and its Allies faced the Soviet Union and the threat of communism for decades after. Comic books during this "Nuclear Era" explore how superheroes reflected American feelings about communism, nuclear weapons, the meaning of family and domestic tranquility, and the role superheroes played in all of it.[38]

One of the first superheroes to directly address anti-communist fervor associated with Sen. Joseph McCarthy was Simon and Kirby's Fighting American, published in 1954 by Prize Comics. McCarthy, who served on the Senate Committee on Government Operations from 1953 to 1954, whipped up an anti-communist frenzy that had both political leaders and the public skeptical of their friends and neighbors and anxious about Soviet infiltration in the United States.[39] Fighting American's stories had five main themes that reflected American fears and anxieties in the first years of the Cold War: domestic foreign spies, organized crime, foreign troops on American soil, worldwide communist sabotage, and the loss of American freedom and ideals.[40] Simon and Kirby both stated their character was dedicated to taking on the "red menace" and were proud to create "the first commie-basher in comics."[41]

The comics that most acted as a mirror for feelings and events of the Cold War in America were the "Fantastic Four" from Marvel Comics. These superheroes who did not act like superheroes explored themes of atomic anxieties, gender roles, the family, science and new technology and communism—all in the first eight issues of a series about four bickering superpowered humans.[42] The first issue of "Fantastic Four" had its origins in the race to get to space, which was an offensive tactic against the Soviet Union and Communism. Brilliant scientist Reed Richards, his girlfriend Susan Storm, her younger brother Johnny Storm, and Reed's best friend Ben Grimm take a prototype spaceship to space to "beat the 'commies.'"[43] Throughout this first issue, Susan worries about the effects of "cosmic rays," which when they go to space, give the four superpowers. Reed becomes Mr. Fantastic and can stretch and twist his body in unnatural ways, Susan gets powers of invisibility, Johnny becomes a human fireball, and Ben transforms into a monstrous, rock-like humanoid with super strength.[44] In comic book historiography, Dr. Reed Richards is considered a "personification of science and technology as an expression of America's greatness" while also reflecting public fears about scientists and technology in the years following the creation of the atomic bomb.[45] This debate over scientists is also reflected again in "Fantastic Four #5," when the group first encounters Doctor Doom, real name Victor von Doom. Doctor Doom is a scientific match for him, but Reed Richards explains that Doctor Doom is only interested in forbidden experiments, magic, and time travel. Doctor Doom is even drawn at a desk with books about "Demons" and "Science and Sorcery" on top.[46] This issue gives the Fantastic Four an arch enemy, but it also explains "that it is not the science, but the scientists, that is good or evil."[47]

Other "Fantastic Four" comics explore the American fear of communist brainwashing and the government's awareness of the effects of the Manhattan Project and the atomic bomb. In "Fantastic Four #2," the group fight the "Skrulls from Outer Space," who can transform themselves into an exact match of any living being. The Skrulls turn themselves into the Fantastic Four and wreak havoc, turning the community against the Fantastic Four. To defeat them, Reed Richards uses hypnotism to imprison the Skrulls and make them transform into cattle.[48] This new fear of brainwashing manifested in American minds in the years following the Korean War, with the worry that good people could be involuntarily turned into communists. The Skrulls also reflected the fear of imposters running rampant in the United States.[49] In a later issue, the Fantastic Four fight the Sub-Mariner when he unleashes an atomic bomb over New York City. The group retaliates with its own bomb, inferring that the "government is not only aware of the intended use of the bomb, but that it is complicit in the bomb's detonation."[50]

The appearance of Marvel Comics' Incredible Hulk and Iron Man around the same time as the Fantastic Four directly reflected American opinions of science and atomic energy and the Vietnam War's role within the overall Cold War era. During the detonation of the experimental bomb, Dr. Bruce Banner is exposed to gamma rays, which give him the ability—or rather, instability—of transforming into the monstrous, super strong Incredible Hulk.[51] Hulk is neither hero nor villain and like nuclear energy itself, "is a complex and often uncontrollable natural force."[52] Hulk's arch enemy, General Thaddeus "Thunderbolt" Ross, wants to contain the nuclear threats, the Hulk, and the military experiments that created him. However, Hulk's stories show the human inability to control human nature and atomic energy.[53] In 1963's "Tales of Suspense #39," Tony Stark and Iron Man are first introduced. Tony Stark is a weapons creator and dealer and is presenting a new weapon to the American war effort in Vietnam. Tony Stark and his group are attacked, he is gravely injured and captured by the "Red Guerilla Tyrant Wong-Chu," and must make a suit of iron to stay alive. Though Tony Stark survives thanks to his genius and technological skill, the early Iron Man stories showed how the Vietnam War made the public doubt America's "military invincibility."[54]

The fear and anxieties of the 1950s gave way to the decades of the ongoing Cold War marked by youth counterculture and malaise. Incredible Hulk and Fantastic Four stories continued to explore national feelings around science, technology, and communism, but also began confronting real-world problems and showcasing the youth point of view of the world. Marvel Comics also added to their list of Cold War comics with Spider-Man in 1962, which when he appeared in "Amazing Fantasy #15," gave teenagers a starring role in a superhero story. The Spider-Man stories also gave America's youth a voice and reflected the tumultuous relationship between teenage immaturity, science-enhanced powers, and community responsibility. The malaise of the 1970s is reflected in prominent characters like the Hulk, Superman, and Iron Man, and new characters like Deathlok and the Inhumans, struggling with who they are and their role in the world. These malaise-themed stories demonstrated that President Jimmy Carter was right in his proclamation that the country was suffering from a "crisis of confidence."[55] The Iron Man "Demon in a Bottle" storyline from 1979 shows Tony Stark struggling with alcoholism, the "Secret Empire" storyline in Captain America comics during 1973 and 1974 allude to President Richard Nixon and Watergate, and Jack Kirby's "The Eternals" stories create a mood of "human insignificance" and complete powerlessness.[56]

The Cold War and other events of the 1970s gave Americans the feeling that the country was on a downward spiral, and comics books reflected that not even superheroes could save the nation and its ideals. As the malaise gave way to the conservative era of President Ronald Reagan and the 1980s, comic book creators crafted and reimagined superheroes as violent vigilante that "no longer exclusively followed the traditional comic book view of right and wrong."[57] In the 1980s and into the 1990s, scholars began studying comic books as historical material and writing of the role these colorful texts played in American culture.[58] At the same time, while some comic characters returned to their 1940s or 1950s innocent roots, new characters emerged that violently "critiqued and criticized" society's direction.[59]

In 1986, two comic series emerged that directly reflected the last years of Cold War anxieties and skepticism and the rise of radical conservativism in America. British writer Alan Moore's "Watchmen" series presents an alternative history where superheroes are real, the United States won the Vietnam War, and Watergate never happened. The superheroes in "Watchmen" are not moral patriots, but rather brooding, costumed vigilantes. As World War III and the Soviet Union loom in the series, Moore explores the fear of "impending atomic doom and how even superheroes appear to be unable to prevent a nuclear holocaust."[60] "Watchmen" showed what a world with unregulated and unsupervised superheroes would be like and how America would react to knowing these heroes could not save them from themselves. With the series' writer, artist, and colorist being British, "Watchmen" was also commentary on how other countries viewed American ideals and culture at the end of the Cold War. One character, Dr. Manhattan, shows a man who's lost his humanity and now embodies the 1980s understanding of nuclear power: "cold, calculating, and extremely dangerous."[61] Dr. Manhattan, named after the Manhattan Project that created the first atomic bomb, is the only character in "Watchman" with superpowers and lives on Mars after allegations that he gave people cancer.[62]

Frank Miller's "Batman: The Dark Knight Returns" also draws on 1980s post-Watergate opinions about political leaders and American society. Contradicting fellow DC character Superman, Batman as The Dark Knight was a billionaire vigilante with no powers but exuding skepticism of the government and promoting individualism above all else.[63] "The Dark Knight Returns" was Miller's view of Reagan-era America told through the lens of a fictional caped crusader fighting Gotham City gangs and old enemies like the Joker and Two-Face. Within this series that eventually pitted Superman against Batman at the request of President Reagan, Miller critiqued the news media, local government and law enforcement corruption, and American culture.[64] Miller's series illustrated what the creator considered acceptable comic tales during the mid-1980s and how Miller concluded that society and superheroes suffer from the same flaws.

In his research of comic books and American society, Jeffrey K. Johnson said Miller showed through "The Dark Knight Returns" that both society and comic book heroes are "overly violent, self-righteous, and self-absorbed, and should not be praised for these qualities."[65]

As the Cold War finally ended and the 1990s began, comic books continued with more violent, vigilante content, but some of the most popular series of this decade focused on characters reimagined for a generation gearing up for a new millennium. The new Spider-Man and X-Men comics that came out in 1990 and 1991 became the most popular of the decade and featured classic superhero style and stories packaged in colorful, flashy packaging.[66] These characters mirrored the hopes of a decade focusing on the future and reflected the "unencumbered energy and enthusiasm" released after the Cold War ended.[67] By the end of the 1990s, Superman—once thought to be invincible and unstoppable—died, the original Spider-Man and Batman quit their superhero jobs, and new publishing houses, characters, and forward-looking stories emerged.[68]

Comic books have been colorful mirrors to America's fears, hopes, desires, and culture since their creations in the early twentieth century. These fictional characters and stories often alluded to or directly addressed current events, figures, and war, and helped shape the country's social history. For readers during times of war, comic books "promote different ideologies or specific economic or political positions," and provided an entertaining, fictional outlet to see their emotions, confusion, and questions portrayed in printed panels.[69] These books depicting the unreal and the fantastic were once considered lowbrow entertainment for children with little educational or historical value. What we can see with comic books published during war, however, is a basis in reality that may not detail exactly how America's conflicts played out but does show how the American public felt about World War I, the Great Depression, World War II, the Cold War, and the beginnings of the War on Terror. Through the lens of comic books, society's feelings about war evolved from patriotism, moral superiority, and fear, to anxiety, skepticism, and eventually relief and hope for a brighter, super heroic future.

Bibliography

Flagg, James Montgomery. *"I Want You."* 1917. Armed Forces History, Division of History of Technology, National Museum of American History, Washington D.C.

Johnson, Jeffrey K. *Super-History: Comic Book Superheroes and American Society, 1938 to the Present.* Jefferson: McFarland & Company, Publishers, 2012.

Kirby, Jack, and Joe Simon. "Captain America #1." NY: Marvel Comics, 1941.

Kirby, Jack, and Joe Simon. "Captain America #2." NY: Marvel Comics, 1941.

Kirby, Jack, and Stan Lee. "Fantastic Four #1-5." NY: Marvel Comics, 1961.

Kirby, Jack, and Stan Lee. "The Incredible Hulk #1." NY: Marvel Comics, 1962.

Lee, Stan, Lieber, Larry, and Don Heck. "Tales of Suspense #39." NY: Marvel Comics, 1959.

Marcus, Edwin, Artist. *The Rainbow*! Europe United States, 1917. [?] Photograph. https://www.loc.gov/item/2016683677/.

Marston, William, and Harry Peter. "Sensation Comics #1." NY: DC Comics, 1941.

Miller, Frank. *Batman: The Dark Knight Returns.* New York: DC Comics, 1986.

Moore, Alan, and Dave Gibbons. *Watchmen.* New York: DC Comics, 1986.

Pustz, Matthew. *Comic Books and American Cultural History: An Anthology.* New York: Continuum International Publishing Group, 2016.

Scott, Cord A. *Comics and Conflict: Patriotism and Propaganda from WWII Through Operation Iraqi Freedom.* Annapolis, MD: Naval Institute Press, 2014.

Tipton, Carrie Allen. 2018. "Snoopy Remembers the Great War." *History Today* 68 (11): 18–20. http://search.ebscohost.com.ezproxy2.apus.edu/login.aspx?direct=true&AuthType=ip&db=aph&AN=132159861&site=ehost-live&scope=site.

York, Chris, and Rafiel York. *Comic Books and the Cold War 1946-1962: Essays on Graphic Treatment of Communism, the Code and Social Concerns.* Jefferson (C.): McFarland, 2012.

Notes

1 Jeffrey K. Johnson, *Super-History: Comic Book Superheroes and American Society*. N.C.: McFarland & Company, Inc., 2012, 2.

2 Cord A. Scott, *Comics and Conflict: Patriotism and Propaganda from WWII Through Operation Iraqi Freedom*. MD: Naval Institute Press, 2014.

3 Ibid.

4 James Montgomery Flagg, *"I Want You."* Washington D.C.: National Museum of American History, 1917.

5 Scott, 4.

6 Ibid, 5.

7 Marcus, Edwin, Artist. *The Rainbow!* Europe United States, 1917. [?] Photograph. https://www.loc.gov/item/2016683677/

8 Scott, 6.

9 Ibid.

10 Carrie Allen Tipton, "Snoopy Remembers the Great War." *History Today* 68, 2011.

11 Ibid.

12 Ibid.

13 Ibid.

14 Scott, 3.

15 Scott, 9.

16 Johnson, 8.

17 Ibid., 21.

18 Johnson, 3.

19 Scott, 3.

20 Johnson, 12.

21 Scott, 3.

22 Ibid., 16.

23 Jack Kirby and Joe Simon. "Captain America #1." NY: Marvel Comics, 1941.

24 Matthew Pustz. *Comic Books and American Cultural History: An Anthology*. NY: Continuum International Publishing Group, 2012, 111.

25 Kirby and Simon, "Captain America #1," 1941.

26 Kirby and Simon, "Captain America #3," 1941.

27 Scott, 25.

28 Ibid.

29 Scott, 12.

30 Ibid., 14.

31 Ibid., 25.

32 William Marston and Harry Peter. "Sensation Comics #1." NY: DC Comics, 1941.

33 Scott, 30.

34 Ibid., xi.

35 Ibid.

36 Scott, 16.

37 Johnson, 3.

38 Ibid.

39 Pustz, 110.

40 Ibid., 113.

41 Ibid.

42 Chris York and Rafiel York. *Comic Books and the Cold War 1946-1962: Essays on Graphic Treatment of Communism, the Code and Social Concerns.* N.C.: McFarland & Company, 2012, 13.

43 Jack Kirby and Stan Lee. "Fantastic Four #1." NY: Marvel Comics, 1961.

44 Ibid.

45 York and York, 207.

46 Kirby and Lee, "Fantastic Four #5," 1963.

47 York and York, 213.

48 Kirby and Lee, "Fantastic Four #2," 1962.

49 York and York, 209.

50 Ibid., 212.

51 Jack Kirby and Stan Lee, "The Incredible Hulk #1." NY: Marvel Comics, 1962.

52 Johnson, 60.

53 Ibid.

54 Pustz, 137.

55 Pustz, 138.

56 Ibid., 144.

57 Johnson, 3.

58 Ibid., 2.

59 Ibid., 3.

60 Johnson, 66.

61 Ibid., 67.

62 Alan Moore and Dave Gibbons. *Watchmen*. NY: DC Comics, 1986.

63 Johnson, 141.

64 Frank Miller. *Batman: The Dark Knight Returns,* (NY: DC Comics) 1986.

65 Johnson, 141.

66 Johnson, 154.

67 Ibid.

68 Ibid., 169.

69 Scott, xi.

The Skagway Commercial Club

Jennifer L. Williams
American Public University

Abstract

The Skagway Commercial Club was formed as a community effort to promote Skagway, Alaska as a travel destination in early 20th century. Using period newspapers and publications, corporate and individual promotional literature, and relevant secondary sources, the article discusses the efforts of the Skagway Commercial Club to promote Skagway as a tourism destination in the first three decades of the twentieth century and evaluates its effectiveness of the Commercial Club in relation to outside advertisements such as cruise ship literature and shop brochures published by individual business owners. While the Club did try to actively promote Skagway during its first two or three years in existence, its efforts were minor compared to the individual efforts by business owners to advertise and promote their own businesses.

Keywords: The Daily Alaskan (newspaper), Martin Itjen, Herman D. Kirmse, Klondike Gold Rush, Skagway Alaska, Skagway Commercial Club, Southeast Alaska, Tourism, White Pass & Yukon Railroad

El Skagway Commercial Club

Resumen

El Skagway Commercial Club se formó como un esfuerzo comunitario para promover Skagway, Alaska, como destino turístico a principios del siglo XX. Utilizando periódicos y publicaciones de época, literatura promocional corporativa e individual, y fuentes secundarias relevantes, el artículo analiza los esfuerzos del Skagway Commercial Club para promover Skagway como un destino turístico en las primeras tres décadas del siglo XX y evalúa su efectividad Club en relación con anuncios externos, como literatura de cruceros y folletos de tiendas publicados por propietarios de negocios individuales. Si bien el Club trató de promover activamente Skagway durante sus primeros dos o tres años de existencia, sus esfuerzos fueron menores en comparación con los esfuerzos individuales de los dueños de negocios para anunciar y promover sus propios negocios.

Palabras clave: The Daily Alaskan (periódico), Martin Itjen, Herman D. Kirmse, Klondike Gold Rush, Skagway Alaska, Skagway Commercial Club, Sureste de Alaska, Turismo, White Pass y Yukon Railroad

斯卡圭商业俱乐部

摘要

20世纪初，阿拉斯加斯卡圭社区创立斯卡圭商业俱乐部（Skagway Commercial Club），将斯卡圭作为旅游目的地加以宣传。通过使用当时的报纸和刊物、企业和个体宣传资料、以及相关二次文献，本文探讨了20世纪前三十年斯卡圭商业俱乐部在将斯卡圭作为旅游目的地加以宣传一事上所作的努力，并评价了与个体企业家出版的游轮资料和商店宣传册等外部广告相比，商业俱乐部所作宣传的有效性。尽管在最开始的两三年里商业俱乐部的确试图积极宣传斯卡圭，但与个体企业家在宣传其各自业务上所作的努力相比，商业俱乐部产生的宣传效果更小。

关键词：阿拉斯加日报（The Daily Alaskan），Martin Itjen，Herman D. Kirmse，克朗代克淘金热，斯卡圭（阿拉斯加），斯卡圭商业俱乐部，阿拉斯加东南部，旅游业，白隘口和育空铁路

As part of the Skagway Chamber of Commerce, the Skagway Commercial Club began with an organizational meeting on June 16, 1909. The sole purpose of the Commercial Club (or the Club) was "aiding the growth and development of Skagway."[1] All citizens were invited to attend the meeting, not just business owners. The Club (or SCC) was not different from other Commercial Clubs in Juneau, Skagway, Petersburg, Wrangell, or Ketchikan that produced promotional literature for tourism and to attract industry to Southeast Alaska, each promoting their location. Sitka and Wrangell were the other two established locations in Southeast Alaska. Sitka functioned at the capital of Russia American until the acquisition of the Alaskan territory by the United States and Wrangell was ruled by the Tlingit, the British (Hudson Bay Company), the Russians, and finally, the United States. Ketchikan started a small salmon canning settlement in the 1870s; Juneau developed because of gold quartz strikes in the 1880s; and Petersburg was established as a Norwegian settlement in 1897. All these locations established Commercial Clubs to market their unique history and location. This article will discuss the efforts of the Skagway Commercial Club (SCC) to promote Skagway as a tourist destination, how these efforts were supplemented by outside sources such as the cruise ship literature and individual shop brochures, and how Skagway compared with other locations in Southeast Alaska.

While the Club was not the only promoter of Skagway's interests, the organization was dominated by businessmen and women in Skagway through the 1920s. Martin Itjen was a very colorful advocate of Skagway's interests, particularly in the 1920s, with his Yellow Bus driving tours in Skagway and a visit to California to promote Southeast Alaska. The White Pass and Yukon Railroad would tout its daily excursion to the Canadian border and back for "day trippers," as the daily visitors were called. Promotional material published by the cruise ship lines described each destination in their travel brochures and they would become more detailed and colorful through the 1920s as towns in Southeast Alaska expanded their excursions. The Club is most often mentioned in the newspapers, so it is a primary focus for this study in the promotional efforts of the Club and its supporters for the first four decades of the 20th century.

Skagway's unique location as one of two entry points to the Klondike Gold Rush, which began in 1896, created a boom town overnight. Dyea, the second location and the starting point of the steep but shorter Chilkoot Pass, sank into insignificance after the Gold Rush ended by 1899, and with the completion of the White Pass & Yukon Railroad to the Canadian interior in 1900.[2] Robert Spude's work on the construction and architecture from 1884–1912 divides Skagway into four distinct construction phases, which is useful to trace the town's ascendancy during the Gold Rush, and its struggles to maintain its relevancy after the decline. The completion of the White Pass and Yukon Railroad was the centerpiece of the town's remarkable resilience. Supplies still needed to reach the British Columbia and Yukon interior so freight, mail, and passengers kept the railroad profitable. Several sources tend to agree that Skagway's tourism industry took off after the White Pass &Yukon Railroad realized that visitors would expand freight and resident passenger trips to the Canadian Interior after the Klondike Gold Rush. However, the creation of a "new" Skagway required civic cooperation and the local businessmen were willing to capitalize on Skagway's natural beauty and Gold Rush history to attract visitors. From a tent city in 1897 to an orderly procession of one-story buildings down Broadway to the multi-tiered saloons, hotels, and businesses just after the turn of the century,[3] Skagway took on the characteristics of permanent town rather than a Gold Rush boom town. By end of the first decade of the 20th century, Skagway's population was 600. While it was no longer the Gold Rush boom town, the economy stabilized, and it emerged as a main tourist attraction in Southeast Alaska.[4]

The leisure travel industry is almost a century and a half old.[5] Taken from the 18th century concept of the Grand European Tour of the very wealthy and the aristocracy, which has its antecedents in the pilgrimages and exploration of the Medieval and Renaissance periods, leisure travel became a marketable industry in the United States after the Industrial Revolution in the 19th century. As more people immigrated or moved into the cities, the populations swelled into factories and industry. The new work schedule, consisting of five days a week and two days for leisure time, allowed for the rising middle class to take time off for travel. Railroads hauled freight and paying passengers into parts of continents still little settled or rarely (if ever) seen by outsiders. Eventually, steamship travel and trans-oceanic luxury liner crossed the open waters, carrying passengers and freight to destinations across the globe. By the middle of the 19th century, established travel tours were available. "Once regular steamship service between several West Coast ports and southeastern Alaska had been established in 1884, a smaller but steadily increasing number of well-to-do Americans began touring the Inside Passage" and tour ships originated from the ports of Seattle, Tacoma, San, Francisco, and Portland.[6]

While it is difficult to get an accurate year to year count of visitors to Skagway (or Southeast Alaska in general), newspapers disclosed numbers for the sake of self-promotion as well as civic pride. For example, on July 18, 1916, the Jefferson of the Pacific Alaska Steamship Company "is scheduled to make this port some time Wednesday morning. Sixty-five round trip excursion tickets to the Summit (White Pass Summit) have been sold by the purser so a large number of tourists are aboard that boat."[7] Skagway, like many locations in Southeast Alaska, began to prepare for the tourist season by mid-March as announcements appeared concerning visitor traffic for the upcoming summer. Skagway's only daily newspaper after 1909 until it ceased publication in the 1920s, *The Daily Alaskan*, published passenger counts from ships expected in port and letters from the steamship company executives on the expectations of the coming season. One of the first mentions of tourism travel was from the *Alaska Traveler's Guide*, a short-lived daily paper published from July 12, 1900 – May 16, 1902, that provided information on Skagway businesses—hotels, restaurants, shops, and mail delivery and city services, and the White Pass & Yukon Railroad schedules. "The Sound (referencing Seattle perhaps) papers say there will be a greatly increased tourist travel this summer. The steamship companies are getting ready for it."[8] *The Interloper*, Skagway's third newspaper, has few extant copies between May 5, 1908 and April 10, 1909. Its pages covered baseball games and tournaments and many of the political issues of the day. City Council meetings were also discussed in this paper but no references to tourism or the promotion of Skagway. Skagway's self-promotion through the Commercial Club and dominance in the cruise ship literature helped the small town become a must-see cruise destination in Southeast Alaska. It would establish Skagway as a primary destination that continues to be popular today.

In the post-Gold Rush era, Skagway wanted to capitalize on the Gold Rush history and the natural beauty of its location at the head of Lynn Canal. Skagway's Chamber of Commerce was formed in 1900 to support existing businesses and attract new businesses to the small town. The *Alaska Traveler's Guide* routinely covered the Chamber's weekly meetings during the paper's existence. "The Chamber is composed of many of Skagway's leading business men" including Dr. L.S. Keller.[9] The stated purpose of the organization was "to promote the general prosperity of the district of Alaska and the city and port of Skagway in particular."[10] Unfortunately, the Chamber records have not survived to indicate the membership or the Chamber's specific involvement in the promotion of Skagway between its founding in 1900 and 1940, the time frame for this article. However, many of the names in connection with the Skagway Commercial Club were also members of the Chamber and the Commercial Club was a broader appeal to all citizens of Skagway, as indicated by articles published in *The Daily Alaskan*, to become involved in the promotion of the town.

Between 1910 and 1914, the Skagway Commercial Club was the most active in the promotion of Skagway as a tourist destination. One of the first acts of the Skagway Commercial Club in 1909 was to offer a prize for the best design to be used on the Commercial Club's stationary masthead. The stationary was intended for "all business men and other residents of Skagway who will use the same" for the promotion of Skagway in regular correspondence, "and assist in advertising and boosting the town ... it must be descriptive of Skagway, conveying the idea that Skagway in the national GATEWAY TO THE INTERIOR, and that there is a greater variety of attractions for tourists here than any other place."[11] Several published reports discuss the use of the promotional stationary by Herman Kirmse, the owner of one of the largest curios stores in Southeast Alaska at the time.[12] By the end of March 1910, several the town's major businesses were ordering Commercial Club stationary, "thus making every letter that they write a traveling advertisement for Skagway."[13]

The greatest effort of promotion for Skagway by the Club came in 1910 with publication of a booklet for distribution. In a January 10, 1910 article, *The Daily Alaskan* noted that in the meeting, "it was decided to have 10,000 booklets printed which will set forth Skagway's advantages and attractions as a tourist resort."[14] The booklet contained photographs of Skagway. "Secretary Muller read a booklet which he had prepared advertising Skagway as a summer tourist resort ... Dyea, Denver Glacier ... Smuggler's Cove ... over the old White Pass trail and to Atlin and

Whitehorse."[15] The booklet's format and information were voted on and accepted at that meeting. An editorial published two days later entitled *Advertising Skagway As A Tourist Resort* about the first meeting of the Club, its formation is "most gratifying to those who have stuck by Skagway through thick and thin" and "it was decided to have 10,000 booklets printed … set forth Skagway's advantages and attractions as a tourist resort" and "should receive the active support of the people of Skagway."[16]

The first three months of 1910 were spent compiling information and asking for block cuts for the publication. The committee responsible for the booklet took subscriptions for the estimated $5,000 publication cost. The committee was made up of photographer H.H. Draper, J.M. Keller, W.C. Blanchard (of the White Pass & Yukon Railroad), and E.L. Miller, all local businessmen or employees of the White Pass & Yukon Railroad. H.H. Draper served as the chairman in the 1910 for the publication. Places of distribution for the booklet included "H.D. Kirmse's Jewelry Store and H.H. Draper's Curio Store."[17] By April's meeting, the Club was discussing the distribution of the advertising booklets, printed by the newspaper office.[18] Residents were encouraged to submit a list of prospective visitors to E.L. Miller so a pamphlet could be mailed to them. H.C. Bundy presented a plan to advertise "the resources of this district as a resort for tourists"[19] at a regular meeting of the organization. After late October, only two other meeting notices were advertised in *The Daily Alaskan*, both delaying any meeting due to a lack of business.

The promotional booklet, simply titled *Skagway, Alaska* was produced by the Skagway Commercial Club. The second page requests that cruise ship passengers "[a]sk the steamship company's agent to tell you all about the stop-over privilege on your tickets. You may remain in Skagway a couple of weeks or more to visit the many and beautiful interesting places in and adjacent to our town."[20] In the first article, the visitor is asked to

> … walk leisurly (sic) down the street and we will stare in surprise and wonder at the fine cosmopolitan shops and stores, and the large and well built hotels, fraternal halls, water works, the electric light and telephone system, the daily newspaper, the government cable, which keeps you in constant touch with all the outer world … Then let us visit the residence streets and see the pretty homes with well-kept lawns and flower gardens, the churches, schools, and the first class hospital, and you will wonder how this little far-away town could improve so rapidly when it did not come into existence until 1898, at which time it was the head-quarters of many eager gold-hunters and prospectors bound for the Klondike and other parts of Alaska, from 5,000 to 10,000 in number, housed in tents, old shacks, and similar other structures providing but scanty shelter.[21]

Source: P277-001-003 Alaska State Library Wickersham State Historic Sites Photo Collection

The article continues to discuss the many shops in Skagway, stating that the visitor may find a variety of travel souvenirs including "brown bear, black bear and polar bear skins ... also nuggets for watch charms, and nuggets made into watch chains, bracelets, stick pins, and brooches ... varieties of cribbage boards and napkin rings, made from the tusks of the Alaskan walrus; moccasins made from the hair seal, and Indian baskets made in every shape and size conceivable."[22] A discussion of the temperate climate is next in the article along with a description of the Skagway gardens as well as the wild berries in the area, and the midnight sun. All these features "help[ed] characterize Skagway as the natural headquarters for tourists."[23]

The booklet continues to describe the trip from Seattle or Vancouver on the spacious and comfortable steamers into Southeast Alaska and briefly mentions other locations that will be visited by the steamship companies, including "Ketchikan, Juneau, Wrangell, Treadwell, and its great gold mines, Haines, Sitka, Killisnoo, the Indian Village Metlakahtla, Fort William H. Seward; also Taku and Muir Glaciers, and miscellaneous other places of interest."[24] An entire article is dedicated to discussing the beauty of Skagway's location at the top of Lynn Canal as well as the mountain climbing, hunting, and fishing expeditions possible during a stay in Skagway. Of course, the summer salmon runs are singled out for specific mention.

Looking south, down Broadway, from 5th Avenue towards the modern cruise ship terminal. When first constructed the WP&YR track ran straight down the center of Broadway. By February 1899 the like reached White Pass summit. By July 1900 a full 110 miles of track had been laid from Skagway Alaska to Carcross in the Yukon Territory. Photo reprinted with the permission of the Municipality of Skagway Visitor Department www.skagway.com.

As a major contributor to the economic well-being of Skagway as a freight hauler to the Canadian Interior, the booklet devotes a short article to the excursions of the White Pass & Yukon Railroad. The railroad was a driving force in Skagway's appeal as additional excursions were developed into the 1920s and 1930s aside from a round-trip ride to the White Pass Summit. The very descriptive article begins with a very brief history of the railroad and the Klondike Gold Rush, stating that

> We will board the train at Broadway station, and after passing through the principal part of the town we cross Skagway river, noisy and icy cold, hurrying on its way to the sea. Soon we pass over the old White Pass trail … You imagine it peopled with all those thousands who toiled and travelled over its rugged paths in 1897 and 1898, the steady streams of gold seekers, pack laden, eager hearted, and buoyed up with the prospects that lured them onward … Just below you lays the old historic White Pass City where 10,000 eager gold seekers camped for brief periods before making the final effort up the canyon; and we see Dead Horse Gulch … where hundreds of horses, overtired and too-heavily ladened, unable to proceed farther, tottered and fell

"In 2005 No. 69 returned to the White Pass route after 49 years of service in Wisconsin and a complete overhaul. Built in 1907 by Baldwin, this 2-8-0 was the biggest steam loco to operate on the White Pass Summit route. No. 69 was named Gila Monster by the US Army in WW2 and converted to an oil burner in 1951. The loco left the White Pass & Yukon Railroad in 1956, sold to the Black Hills Central Railway in South Dakota where it was renamed Klondike Casey. In 1973 it became Nebraska Midland No. 69 where it served until 1990. The WP&YR bought the locomotive back in 2001 and sent it to the Midwest loco works for overhaul." Source: Railways Illustrated. The White Pass and Yukon Railway—The railway built of gold. October 2005.

over the edge of the precipitous cliffs into the depths of the dark canyons beneath.[25]

An excursion on the White Pass & Yukon Railroad could end at the United States—Canadian border, or the traveler could continue "on to Caribou, a town of the Yukon Territory, and only 69 miles distant from Skagway, where you may board the steamer "Gleaner" for the Atlin Gold Fields."[26] The booklet concludes with brief one page descriptions of Skagway accommodations, trips to Denver Glacier, and a listing of community and civic organizations and schools, and a two page article on renting or taking a motorboat trip along with the locations available to visit including Haines.[27] The photography of H.H. Draper, who also spent a season photographing the Klondike Gold Rush and stampeders, highlights the main articles in the booklet. Indeed, Skagway is well represented between the articles and the photography. It is a neatly designed booklet to showcase the positive attributes of the location and the town.

By 1911, the promotion of Skagway as a tourist destination by the Club had begun to lag with the publication of the promotional booklet in the previous year. However, the Commercial Club encouraged Skagway residents to purchase subscriptions to the *Alaska-Yukon Magazine* in July after a visit from A. F. Holloway, a representative of the magazine. In exchange, "the magazine offers to give a six-page illustrated write-up of Skagway, and afterward one page per month throughout the year."[28] The Club cited that the Ketchikan Commercial Club was able to raise 125 subscriptions, purchased by Ketchikan residents, in a few days. While the promotion of the town was not the only concern of the Club,[29] the efforts at promotion did languish, or at least there were fewer articles in the newspaper. By July, an unsigned editorial, possibly written by paper publisher Dr. L. S. Keller (he operated Keller Drug Store with his brother)[30] or picked up from other shared editorials in other newspapers, wondered why there were not efforts to promoting Skagway with tourism season in full swing. The editorial stated, in part, that "The Commercial Club at the present has its organization, its officers, and its meeting place, why doesn't it get busy? The members of the Club should hold a meeting and devise some way of distributing the remaining booklets ... July, August, and September are the months of the year for tourist travel."[31] The balance of the year mentions the Commercial Club only in an advertisement to stock up on the Club's stationary.

Between 1912–1914, few references to the Skagway Commercial Club appeared in *The Daily Alaskan*. As the only daily newspaper in Skagway since 1909, it was the perfect vehicle to inform the town of the efforts to promote business or take up the cause of the lack of mail service on the Upper Lynn Canal run from Juneau. One unsigned editorial referenced the Club, commenting on the visiting Association of Funeral Directors by stating that "it will be up to Skagway to furnish a subject (cadaver) upon which they may show us the latest wrinkles in embalming (sic) and

Southbound, en route to Skagway, from White Pass, Locomotive No. 69 exits the Tunnel Mountain tunnel (elevation 2,275 ft) at mile marker No. 16. The wooden trestle, later reinforced with steel pilings, spans the yawning chasm over Glacier Gorge 1,000 feet above the gulch below. This photo and this Journal's cover photo are reprinted with the permission of White Pass & Yukon Route, www.wpyr.com.

obsequious equipment. The Skagway Commercial Club is perhaps the most fitting body that could be secured for the occasion."[32] The Club was a dead organization in the opinion of the editorial writer.

Finally, in July 1915, a front-page article announced the reorganization of the Skagway Commercial Club. Colonel W. L. Stevenson, who served on board of the Bank of Alaska, was elected chairman and wanted to take advantage of "every opportunity to increase Skagway's desirability and fame as a tourist resort."[33] According to the article, there was a scheme by an unnamed group to build hotels and resorts all over Alaska but it came to nothing.[34] Three days later, the Club began their new boosting efforts by addressing the issues of the damaged Skagway River bridge. Addressing such infrastructure issues was important. While a road over the mountains into British Columbia was not yet constructed, houses and businesses were located across the river at 22nd Street, the current bridge location. In a recap of the previous meeting on September 16, 1915, a special committee formed to "investigate into the matter of the removal or razing of the unsightly and dilapidated buildings in the section of town lying south of Ninth Street."[35] The Club also asked the city council for assistance to improve the appearance of the town so visitors would leave with a favorable impression of Skagway.[36] The previously mentioned bridge over the Skagway River was rebuilt in 1915, largely by the efforts of the Club to make the necessary contacts and approve the contracts and plans. In addition, the Club took up preparations for Alaska's semi-centenary celebration in 1917 in Ketchikan.[37]

The preparations for the Alaskan semi-centenary were not well covered in *The Daily Alaskan*. The Alaska Bureau of the Seattle Chamber of Commerce printed a four-page advertisement with travel options to promote to Alaska on its fiftieth anniversary. A Mr. Person was "on a tour of Alaska to learn the wishes of the Alaskans as to the observance in 1917 of the fiftieth anniversary of the acquisition of Alaska, so that the Alaska Bureau of the Seattle Chamber of Commerce can plan a campaign of publicity and boost."[38] The two tours offered for the fiftieth anniversary were the Grand Tour and the Coast Tour. The Grand Tour covered all Southeast Alaska and the rest of coastal Alaska including Nome and the Yukon Interior, "requiring fifty days, party limited to 100."[39] The Coast Tour covered "southeast and south coasts as far west as Cook Inlet, requiring 21 days for the round trip, party limited to 240, including those making the grand tour."[40] Skagway is mentioned only briefly, as are the other destinations of the respective tours, and travelers will make the round trip to Summit Pass on the White Pass & Yukon Railroad.[41] The promotion or announcement of visitors from this tour is absent from *The Daily Alaskan* in 1917. The Seattle Chamber of Commerce continued its efforts to promote tourism to Alaska in general through "its tourist booklet for national distribution and it prominently features Alaska excursions."[42]

To facilitate longer visits to Skagway, the Club sent letters to the major shipping companies that served the town—Pacific Coast Steamship Company, Canadian Pacific Steamship Company, and Alaska Steamship Company. A general response from the vice-president of the Alaska Steamship Company stated that the matter would be given consideration. A more lengthy and detailed response from C.D. Duncan, passenger traffic manager, of the Pacific Coast Steamship Company, explained their decision-making process and their effort to facilitate lengthy stopovers in Alaska. "Throughout 1914 and 1915 our excursion tickets to Alaska have carried stopover privileges … The matter of lay-over time allowed our steamers … are arranged to meet ride conditions and various port calls enroute."[43] In a later edition, a letter from E.C. Ward of the Pacific Coast Steamship Company was reproduced concerning the amendment of ships scheduled to allow for longer stopover times. "I will write you later … after we have had an opportunity of considering our schedule for the next season."[44] The Canadian Pacific Railroad response was somewhat similar to the Pacific Coast Steamship Company's response in that "careful consideration with a view to meeting your wishes and at the same time serving the convenience of the tourists visiting Alaska"[45] and it was added that the upcoming 1916 schedule would not change from previous years.

In 1916, the Club became active again, planning for the upcoming tourist season. Because the meeting notes are not extant, the specifics of the meetings are unknown, and it is not clear who submitted summary articles to the *Daily Alaskan* because there is no by-line. It is possible that Dr. Keller, the paper's editor, wrote the summary articles for the paper as no other staff is listed.[46] In this same edition calling for the meeting on the upcoming season, an unsigned editorial, Tourist Trade, outlined how to meet the expectations of the tourist. Since Keller also owned a shop that also sold curios for the tourism trade, he did have a vested interest in the promotion of Skagway to increase visitation. "It behooves us to make preparations for this moving ride of summer tourists," the article exhorts, and offers suggestions such as "Merchants should see that employes (sic) are well informed about Alaska. Be ready and willing to give information and a helping hand to our visitors."[47]

One of the last promotional contests sponsored by the Club was advertised in March 1917 for the "two best discriptive (sic) articles describing Skagway and vicinity."[48] The article must be descriptive of the gardens, climate, hotels and restaurants, accommodations, trains, "and other features of merit and interest to tourists."[49] The manuscript became properly of the Club for use in future promotions. The newspaper would become silent on promotional efforts for the rest of 1917, despite the importance of the fiftieth anniversary of Alaskan's acquisition.

By 1919, the Skagway Commercial Club is rarely mentioned in *The Daily Alaskan*. It is not known if the Club disbanded or simply failed to meet and faded from importance in the promotion of Skagway due to the abundance of cruise line literature or individual promoters. The most well-known Skagway promoter at that time was Martin Itjen. As local historian Frank Norris states, "Itjen's interest in the tourist industry developed slowly over the years. Skagway has enjoyed some summer tourism ever since 1898, and Itjen worked as a hack driver as early as 1915. He liked tourists and had such a facility for describing the area to visitors that his services were in increasing demand on the few summer days when tourist steamers called at Skagway."[50]

Itjen visited actress Mae West in California to promote his streetcar services in 1935 and operated his streetcar tour, converted from a truck wagon used for transporting coal for President Warren G. Harding's 1923 visit, until 1942. His tour included sites such as Skagway's beautiful gardens, the Gold Rush cemetery (Itjen was the caretaker), and Pullen House, which was one of the best hotels in Alaska, and the notorious Soapy Smith's tavern. Norris roundly credits Itjen with saving some of Skagway's historic past through his entertaining and educational streetcar tours.[51]

The only issue that was concerning the Club in 1920 was the passage of the legislation known as the Jones Act, which restricted freight shipments from foreign vessels. "The Skagway Commercial Club (in a letter to the Juneau Empire) strenuously protests against the passage of any bill that will curtail steamship service to Alaska. Senator Jones' amendment to H.R. 10, 378 providing for the elimination of Canadian steamship service will injure busines interests of entire Southeast Alaska."[52] The main concern of Club, according to an earlier editorial, was a new shipping tax that would be levied on Canadian lines. The editorial stated that it was simply a tax that American shipping lines were already paying, "while Canadian ships come and go without charge … It is not likely that a tax of $14,000 a year would cause Canadian lines to quit operations in Alaskan waters."[53] In 1921 and 1922, very little activity toward promoting Skagway was published despite increasing numbers of visitors. In 1922, the only specific mention of the Club is due to the arrest of the Club president, Colonel W. L. Stevenson, and a brief article on the incident of apparently mistaken identity.[54] There were several resolutions passed[55] and the issue of the foot bridge over the Skagway River at Fourth Street was a concern.[56] After 1923, any search for the Skagway Commercial Club comes up empty and *The Daily Alaskan* ceased publication in 1924.

The Skagway Commercial Club was formed to promote Skagway to summer tourists, creating an image of Skagway that capitalized on its stunning and beautiful location at top of Lynn Canal and the historic point of entry for the stampeders on their way to the Yukon interior in search of gold. Although made up a businessmen and women such as Herman Kirmse, the Keller Brothers, and Martin Itjen, and some local citizens, it did not adequately function as a promotional organization for Skagway. It languished for unknown reasons for years at a time, or at least there was no indication of its meetings in the local newspaper. The Club considered ways to make Skagway more attractive for residents and visitors by demolishing blighted buildings and other important aspects of life in Skagway so, the Club was very active in the community. Its existence was part of the need to capitalize on Skagway's location and history to gain economic stability and provide a unique experience that was not available in other locations such as the White Pass & Yukon Railroad excursions and the stories of its colorful past related to the Klondike Gold Rush history.

Bibliography

The Alaska Daily Empire, April 10, 1920. The *Empire* still operates in Juneau today.

The Alaska Daily Empire, May 18, 1920.

The Alaska Traveler's Guide, July 12, 1900.

Alaska Traveler's Guide, March 3, 1901.

Campbell, Robert. *In Darkest Alaska: Travel and Empire Along the Inside Passage.* Philadelphia: University of Pennsylvania Press, 2008.

The Constitution and By-Laws of the Skagway Chamber of Commerce. Skagway, AK: The Daily Alaskan Print, 1900.

The Daily Alaskan, June 16, 1909.

The Daily Alaskan, December 27, 1909.

The Daily Alaskan, January 10, 1910.

The Daily Alaskan, January 12, 1910.

The Daily Alaskan, January 20, 1910.

The Daily Alaskan, March 31, 1910.

The Daily Alaskan, April 17, 1910.

The Daily Alaskan, April 18, 1910.

The Daily Alaskan, October 5, 1910.

The Daily Alaskan, March 29, 1911.

The Daily Alaskan, April 5, 1911.

The Daily Alaskan, July 11, 1911.

The Daily Alaskan, July 25, 1911.

The Daily Alaskan, April 22, 1913.

The Daily Alaskan, July 9, 1915.

The Daily Alaskan, July 28, 1915.

The Daily Alaskan, September 16, 1915.

The Daily Alaskan, November 30, 1915.

The Daily Alaskan, December 2, 1915.

The Daily Alaskan, December 13, 1915.

The Daily Alaskan, July 18, 1916.

The Daily Alaskan, March 19, 1917.

The Daily Alaskan, February 2, 1922.

The Daily Alaskan, February 4, 1922.

The Daily Alaskan, March 30, 1922.

Kan, Sergei. "It's Only Half a Mile from Savagery to Civilization": American Tourists and the Southeastern Alaska Natives in the Late 19th Century" in *Coming to Shore: Northwest Coast Ethnology, Traditions, and Visions*, edited by Marie Mauze, Michael E. Harkin, and Sergei Kan. Lincoln: University of Nebraska Press, 2004.

Norris, Frank. "Martin Itjen—the star of the Skagway Streetcar." Bob Wieking, 2011, September 26, 2020. http://martinitjen.com/article4.html.

Seattle Chamber of Commerce. *Alaska To Participate in Alaska's Semi-Centennial Celebrations*. Seattle, 1917.

Skagway Commercial Club. *Skagway Alaska*, Skagway, Alaska: The Daily Alaskan Print, 1910.

Spude, Robert. *Skagway District of Alaska, 1884-1912: Building the Gateway to the Klondike*. Fairbanks, AK: University of Alaska, 1983.

The Stroller's Weekly, January 28, 1922.

Tourist Trade, *The Daily Alaskan*, March 18, 1916.

Notes

1 *The Daily Alaskan*, June 16, 1909, 1.

2 For a comprehensive understanding of the history of Alaska history and the Klondike Gold Rush and the growth of Skagway and Dyea, there are several good secondary sources available. *The Alaska Anthology*, edited by Stephen Haycox and Mary Childers Mangusso provides a basic understanding into Alaska history. *Russians in Alaska, 1732-1867* by Lydia Black provides a comprehensive look at the Russian involvement in all of Alaska, not just in Southeast. *Klondike Fever* and *Klondike: The Last Great Gold Rush, 1896-1899* by Pierre Berton, *Klondike Gold* by Charlotte Jones, and *Good Time Girls* by Lael Morgan. Roy Minter's *The White Pass* is a comprehensive look at the construction of the White Pass and Yukon Railroad. A very interesting primary source is Adney Tappan's *The Klondike Stampede*. The article focuses on the time after the Gold

49 *The Daily Alaskan*, 4.

50 Frank Norris, "Martin Itjen—the star of the Skagway Streetcar," Bob Wieking, 2011, September 26, 2020, http://martinitjen.com/article4.html.

51 Norris, http://martinitjen.com/article4.html.

52 *The Alaska Daily Empire*, May 18, 1920, 7. As a side note, the newspaper still operates in Juneau today.

53 *The Alaska Daily Empire*, April 10, 1920, 4.

54 *The Daily Alaskan*, February 2, 1922, 4.

55 *The Daily Alaskan*, March 30, 1922, 2.

56 *The Daily Alaskan*, February 4, 1992, 4.

Why the British Lost the American Revolution

Gerald J. Krieger
American Military University

Abstract

The reasons behind the British loss of the American colonies during the American Revolution remain a subject of debate among scholars. How could the most powerful maritime empire in the world lose to an underequipped and poorly trained army? The crux of the conundrum for King George III, the Prime Minister, Lord Frederick North, and members of Parliament in London was that they failed to properly grasp the political complexities in the colonies. This drove strategic errors, operational miscalculations, and ultimately, undermined confidence in leadership. This paper reviews six factors that help explain what went wrong in London in North America. Today, the British dilemma in North America would be categorized as a "wicked problem," or one in which there is no ideal solution, only varying solutions that might create other challenges.

Keywords: British, American Revolution, North America, leadership, communication, Cornwallis, British failure, policies

Por qué los británicos perdieron la revolución estadounidense

Resumen

Las razones detrás de la pérdida británica de las colonias estadounidenses durante la Revolución Estadounidense siguen siendo un tema de debate entre los académicos. ¿Cómo podría el imperio marítimo más poderoso del mundo perder ante un ejército mal equipado y mal entrenado? El quid del enigma para el rey Jorge III, el primer ministro Lord Frederick North y los miembros del Parlamento en Londres fue que no lograron comprender adecuadamente las complejidades políticas de las colonias. Esto generó errores estratégicos, errores de cálculo operativos y, en última instancia, socavó la confianza en el liderazgo. Este artículo revisa seis factores que ayudan a explicar lo que salió mal en Londres en América del Norte. Hoy en día, el dilema británico en América del Norte se categorizaría como un "problema perverso", o uno en el que no hay una solución ideal, solo soluciones variables que podrían crear otros desafíos.

Palabras clave: Británico, Revolución Americana, Norteamérica, liderazgo, comunicación, Cornwallis, fracaso británico, políticas

为何英国人在美国革命中战败

摘要

美国革命期间英国失去美国殖民地背后的原因仍然是学者辩论的主题。全世界最强大的海上帝国如何会败给装备不足和训练欠佳的军队？对国家乔治三世、英国首相、伯爵腓特烈·诺斯、以及伦敦议会成员而言，这个难题的关键在于，他们没有正确把握殖民地的政治复杂性。这导致了战略失误、操作计算错误、并最终削弱了对领导力的信心。本文审视了6个因素，这些因素帮助解释了伦敦方面在北美出了什么差错。如今，北美的英国困境能被归类为一个"棘手问题"，或一个不存在完美解决措施（只能产生其他挑战）的问题。

关键词：英国人，美国革命，北美，领导力，传播，康沃利斯（Cornwallis），英国战败，政策

The reasons behind the British loss of its American colonies during the American Revolution is still the subject of debate among scholars. How could the most powerful maritime empires in the world lose to an underequipped and poorly trained army? The criticisms began even before the war concluded, focusing on the actions of both military and civilian leadership. As historian Dan Morrill pointed out, the nascent American army had no professional military organization, no manufacturing to speak of, challenging the "greatest military power in the world. Great Britain had an army of 50,000 strong, and the greatest navy afloat."[1] However, this is a misplaced criticism. King George III, the Prime Minister, Lord Frederick North, and members of Parliament sent some of the best military leaders to North America, though a few Admirals were too far along in their careers, and entrenched in antiquated tactics, to provide any meaningful support.

Surrender of Cornwallis. Print of Cornwallis handing his sword to Washington. The American troops stand on the left, the British on the right. The French fleet and the wall of the fort at Yorktown are in the background. In the right foreground are a cannon and a drum. Harry T. Peters "America on Stone" Lithography Collection, National Museum of American History.[2]

The problem in North America was complex, and British disadvantages plentiful, with London's errors only exacerbating the situation. Acclaimed historian Robert Middlekauff captured the British dilemma well. He writes, "The British faced problems in the war unlike any they had ever faced, and as rich as their past was, it furnished only limited guidance . . . The war was a civil war against a people in thirteen colonies who gained determination as they fought and sacrificed."[3] Lord North and the American Secretary of State for America, Lord George Germain, attempted to fight a traditional eighteenth-century war as they did in previous wars in Europe, though they discovered that North America was very different. It is true that several British officers fought on the continent earlier during the Seven Years' War (1754-1763), though most retained their European conventions of warfare. General George Washington, along with most Continental generals, sought to engage the British conventionally, though the real struggle was in rural areas and backcountry, where irregular partisan militia harassed and wore down the British army. This type of engagement, *petite guerre,* or literally "small war," was elusive and transient, as small guerrilla units appeared and disappeared quickly and unpredictably concentrating on small guerrilla units that would appear, and then disappear quickly. The British were unprepared for this type of warfare. This generated significant problems for British commanders, dictating tactical changes in the British army. The adjustments were gradual, though the transition from "old world" to "new world" warfare took place in the British ranks during the first few years of the war.[4] However, the partisan militia was a conundrum that the British never fully had an answer for, other than dispatching cavalry officers such as the infamous Lieutenant Colonel Banastre Tarleton.

Today, the British dilemma in North America would be categorized as a "wicked problem," or one in which there is no ideal solution, only varying solutions that might create other challenges. The crux of the conundrum for leaders in London was that they failed to properly grasp the political complexities in the colonies. This drove strategic errors, operational miscalculations, and ultimately, undermined confidence in leadership.[5] Six broad areas must be addressed to frame a discussion of what went wrong for the British in the American colonies. They are:

1. The complexity of fighting and sustaining an army at a distance
2. Communication across the Atlantic
3. Assumptions about the scale and nature of the insurrection
4. Policies framed to shape colonies behavior
5. Structure of the British government, or command and control
6. Financial challenges for England

This essay will elaborate on each of these points to illustrate the complexity and multifaceted challenges behind the British failure in the American colonies. A conclusion will capture the British dilemma and argue that they cut their losses, expanding their empire while eliminating the unsolvable "American problem."

The distance between Boston and England is roughly 3,200 nautical miles, requiring a minimum of six weeks of travel by ship, perhaps longer due to inclement weather and currents. Most of the military supplies for the British army were shipped from various ports in England and Ireland. They did not come from the colonies. However, there were some supplies procured from the colonies such as hay, though this was largely to supplement shipments from the mother country. In 1775, London established contracts for seven companies to supply a thousand tons of food a month to provision the garrisons in North America.[6] They typically fell short, delivering supplies in poor condition, improperly sealed and packaged, leading to spoilage. It was common for supply ships to arrive at American ports filled with rodents that had devoured and ruined the shipments. It was also typical for ships to arrive with moldy or weevil-infested bread, rotten potatoes and vegetables, and dead livestock. For example, in 1775, supply ships arrived in Boston from Ireland and England with significant damage; there were 5,200 barrels of unusable flour among other spoilage.[7] British contractors in America were charged with maintaining a six-month stockpile of reserve in

Boston, though they rarely met the requirement. It was typical for the British army to have no more than thirty days supply consistently throughout the war.[8] Sustaining the army was one challenge; moving it was even more of a logistics nightmare. Transportation of supplies, equipment, and troops was always difficult. To cite one example, General William Howe calculated that to move his thirty-two regiments outside of Boston, he would need 3,662 horses, with 50 tons of hay and oats *daily*, which was significantly more than the British had on hand.[9] This was an annoyance for British officers throughout the war in North America, generating complaints from many, while providing validation for requests to delay campaigns. For example, General Sir Henry Clinton wrote about the challenges of his campaigns after the war. He often mentioned provision shortages as the cause of delaying operations.[10]

The distance across the Atlantic also compounded communication problems. Instructions would arrive months too late, requests for troops for upcoming campaigns would arrive, while troops were dispatched only to miss the narrow campaign window in the north. Due to the changing nature of war in the colonies, timely communication was crucial to coordination across the Atlantic. As Michael Pearson notes, "[T]he appalling communications problem was the one aspect that helped whittle down the advantages of the superior British strength and resources."[11] The British maintained the most powerful navy in the world, though they did not have the largest army. They had to use their limited supply of men sparingly and wisely, which was difficult, considering the vast coastline of North America. The net result was that orders and reports were always months after the fact and could scarcely keep up with the rapidly evolving requirements on the battlefield.

Misplaced assumptions regarding the number of Loyalists who supported King George III was a consistent problem throughout the war. After years of frustration in the northern and middle colonies, reports poured into London about a large number of Loyalists in the south. This led Lord George Germain, British Secretary of State for America, to direct what ultimately became a disastrous attempt to conquer the southern colonies. His "Americanization" of the war meant that loyal Americans would maintain security and policing duties, while the British regulars would clear towns of rebels. The soldiers would eliminate or remove the rebels from an area to ensure that the local authorities could maintain control. Then, they would move to another region. The British finally realized that the large number of Loyalists who were in the southern colonies failed to materialize. This prompted General Lord Charles Cornwallis to abandon the Carolinas for Virginia (after losing a large part of his army during the Battle of Guilford Courthouse). As O'Shaughnessy observes, "Indeed, loyalties were never static and they continued to change, but to the disadvantage of the British."[12] The British failed to grasp that actions conducted "in the name of the King" continually eroded and shifted supporters away from the Crown.

General Charles Cornwallis, 1st Marquis and 2nd Earl Cornwallis, 1738–1805. Artist: John Jones, 1745–1797. The National Portrait Gallery, Smithsonian Institution. Gift of Monroe H. Fabian, 1793.[13]

Cornwallis learned too late that the militia, although not as dependable as many Continental officers would have liked, were effective in their way because they were adept at moving in remote regions in ways a conventional army did not. He would conclude that militia were "the most troublesome and predictable elements in a confusing war."[14] The militia and partisan leaders eroded the confidence of Tory citizens and challenged the British to protect their loyal subjects. Even worse, many Loyalists were determined to exact revenge against their Patriot neighbors. This violence produced vicious retaliation on both sides.[15] This factor ultimately undermined all British efforts for stability in America. This drove uncommitted locals to the Patriot cause.

The structure of the British government also greatly hindered the flow of information. In London, the British Secretary of War was responsible for the army, yet he was not invited to key cabinet meetings during discussions of policy in North America.[16] This created a "fog of war" that was disastrous for planning strategy in America. There were other issues with complex and opaque reporting and sharing information. Intelligence was not shared among cabinet members. Some leaders were not rigorous in capturing the intelligence of potential enemy fleets. For example, Lord Sandwich, the First Lord of the Admiralty, was not aggressive when it came to intelligence regarding the movement of the French Navy. This information was vital to operations for London, given that the few ships they had were stretched around the globe, requiring close and exacting stewardship. This was a consistent problem, undermining the overall British efforts in all colonies. For example, Sandwich allowed French warships to leave without receiving alerts when they went to sea for the West Indies.[17] At best, coordination among the various departments of the eighteenth-century British government was fractured and grossly ineffective.[18] There were divergent opinions and a lack of communication among these departments, which created a fog of strategic priorities that might vary by the campaign season. Under the most ideal conditions, these challenges would have hampered the best military leaders.

The overall policy of taxing Americans centered around generating revenue in the colonies, though what was collected in the colonies was insignificant. The real value of the American colonies was a lucrative trade business. Parliament and King George III overlooked this to force the colonies to submit to their authority. Edmund Burke, one of the most eloquent speakers in Parliament, argued against the folly of taxes when the real profit was in trade. He highlighted the growth of exports from Great Britain to North American and the West Indies, which rose from £500,000 in 1704 to nearly £5,000,000 in 1772.[19] His argument fell on deaf ears. Merchants in London also began to complain in 1775, when exports to North America dropped to £220,000, because they had been as high as £3 million the previous year.[20] The politicians did not listen and were intent on making the rebel Americans follow their policies.

Policies designed to discourage rebellion isolated those who were uncommitted and pushed colonists to the rebel cause. Furthermore, the British abandoned areas and could not protect Loyalists in the country or once they left key cities. As just one of many examples where British policy worked against them, we can look at England's efforts in the Carolinas. For example, Lieutenant Colonel Lord Francis Rawdon led the Royal Volunteers in the Carolinas and began experiencing issues of desertion. His energetic response was to issue a proclamation that any civilian assisting his soldiers would be flogged and sent to the West Indies.[21] Rawdon's harsh proclamation, naturally, worked against him, turning more people who had been neutral against the British, and also further accelerated the desertion of his men. This was true in all the colonies, reflecting misguided assumptions from Loyalist leaders as well as the British. Policy undermined their cause, driving more of the population into the arms of the rebels.

The greatest challenge with British policies in the colonies was rooted in the fact that for almost a century, the British maintained a "hands-off" approach to affairs in North America. The colonies became more independent and less interested in centralized authority. This was clear long before the American Revolution, as all colonies voted against the Albany Plan of 1754. This almost foreshadowed their rebellion against the authority of Parliament. The type of people who came to America is important. People left Great Britain for the colonies to strike out on their own. They were more independently minded than many other groups, which stemmed from their past and how the British colonized new territory. Britain's method of colonization was very "laissez-faire," almost setting the stage by allowing colonies to act independently. The British colonies in America were formed by unique groups of people who were exposed to the violence of the wilderness, while also trapped in an "ideologically polarized period in Western history."[22] This translated to an independent spirit and Lockean notions that rulers were beholden to the ruled. This sense of self-governance lasted until 1775, when the British attempts to yoke the colonies backfired, with disastrous consequences.

While criticism of Britain's failure during the American Revolution is anachronistic, it is worthy to at least review the thoughts of the British who fought in North America to better understand their perspective. Charles Stedman, a former British officer during the war, serving most notably under General Charles Cornwallis, wrote a history of the war, *The History of the Origin, Progress, and Termination of the American War in Two Volumes*, published in 1794. In it, Stedman claims the British lost the war for a few reasons. He wrote that "the narrow views of ministers at home[,] and the misconduct of certain commanders abroad, through a serious of pusillanimity, procrastination, discord, and folly" generated the downfall of England in North America.[23] Finger-pointing was common, and he goes further to refer to the British minister, without naming him. He appears to point the finger at Lord George Germain, writing that he did not possess the genius required to solve the problem, though he does admit that Great Britain had several disadvantages.[24] As John Pancake succinctly pointed out, one cannot blame Germain for the failure of any specific campaign or even the war, without recognizing that it had to be conducted within the stringent confines of British politics.[25] Based on limited communication and incomplete records, it is not hard to see why Stedman did not have a more complete picture of the events that he was caught up in. Some notes and correspondence would not be located and published until the nineteenth century. However, he did recognize that the problem was complex.

Great Britain did not have naval resources due to financial constraints imposed by the Seven Years' War. Consequently, they had to make cuts to their navy, which impacted English abilities to patrol the American coast. London was accustomed to conquering islands. This was well within their wheelhouse as a naval power. However, the small English army was not sufficient to occupy large territories (or land masses) that required significant troop assets. To put it differently, as historian Andrew O'Shaughnessy succinctly states, "Britain had an army of conquest, but not an army of occupation."[26] Throughout the conflict, England could capture major cities, though smaller towns and the backcountry required significantly more troops. Similarly, due to financial cuts, the British navy was reduced after the Seven Years' War, with the "rebuild" not completed until 1778; even then, the lack of vessels meant that blocks were drastically ineffective along the vast American coast.[27] To exercise the authority of Parliament, England killed the "golden goose," which was British trade with North America, while incurring significant debt in the process.

The sheer scale of the distance across the Atlantic exacerbated logistics support for the army, while greatly hampering communication between leaders in London and those in North America. Throughout much of the war in North America, the British army often did not have more than thirty-day supplies, dictating that they forage the land and take what they needed from local farmers when they elected to go on a campaign. This worked against them. The structure of the British government obfuscated clear and concise objectives, while the organization of Parliament meant that some key leaders were not involved in meetings, which would have enhanced communication. England was still recovering from the Seven Years' War, and not in a financial position to field a large army and scale up the construction of precious and expensive ships of the line.

O'Shaughnessy rightly concluded that British leaders were mistakenly held responsible for England's defeat, being criticized for either being too bold or overly cautious. However, this is misplaced. London failed, "not as a result of incompetence and blunder, but because of insufficient resources, the unanticipated lack of Loyalist support, and the popularity of the Revolution."[28] This might be summarized as financial shortfalls, bad assumptions, and policies that drove the popularity of the revolution. Also important and crucial were three other elements. The distance and scale of waging and supporting a war on the other side of the Atlantic, compounded by communication problems, exacerbated by the structure of the British government, must be added to O'Shaughnessy's list. He also shrewdly noted that the men who lost North America also retained Canada, grew the Empire in India, and retained key possessions around the globe.[29] France and Spain did not get much from the treaty because of British victories late in the war in the West Indies, India, and at Gibraltar.[30] The winners were America and England. The most important issue to England was ensuring its dominance over the maritime domain. All countries involved in the Treaty of Paris of 1783 reaffirmed English rights to stop and inspect neutral ships, the basis for their economic warfare, ensuring they maintained the balance of power around the globe.[31] With a hint at conducting a war against a large population, Stedman admits that no contemporary army would have been successful "in a country where the people are tolerably united."[32] At the time, even the British realized that the problem in America was wicked.

Bibliography

Allison, David K & Ferreiro, Larrie D., Eds. *American Revolution: A World War.* Washington, D.C.: Smithsonian Books, 2018.

Atkinson, Rick. *The British Are Coming: The War for America, Lexington to Princeton, 1775-1777.* New York: Henry Holt & Company, 2019. Kindle.

Brumwell, Stephen. *Redcoats: The British Soldier and War in the Americas, 1755-1763.* New York: Cambridge University Press, 2002.

Middlekauff, Robert Middlekauff. *The Glorious Cause: The American Revolution: 1763-1789.* New York: Oxford University Press, 2005.

Morrill, Dan L. *Southern Campaigns of the American Revolution.* Baltimore: The Nautical & Aviation Publishing, 1993.

O'Shaughnessy, Andrew Jackson. *The Men Who Lost America: British Leadership, the American Revolution, and the Fate of the Empire.* New Haven: Yale University Press, 2013.

Pancake, John S. *1777: The Year of the Hangman.* Tuscaloosa, Alabama: The University of Alabama Press, 1977.

Pearson, Michael. *Those Damned Rebels: The American Revolution as Seen Through British Eyes.* Boston: Da Capo Press, 1972.

Shy, John. *A People Numerous and Armed: Reflections on the Military Struggle for American Independence.* Rev. ed. Ann Arbor, Michigan: The University of Michigan Press, 1990.

Stedman, Charles. *The History of the Origin, Progress, and Termination of the American War in Two Volumes vol.1, 1794*. Gale Reprint. New York: Creative Media Partners, 2012.

Tuchman, Barbara W. *The First Salute: A View of the American Revolution*. New York: Ballantine Books, 1988.

Willcox, William B. Willcox, ed. *The American Rebellion: Sir Henry Clinton's Narrative of his Campaigns, 1775-1782, with an Appendix of Original Documents*. New Haven: Yale University Press, 1954.

Notes

1 Dan L. Morrill, *Southern Campaigns of the American Revolution* (Baltimore: The Nautical & Aviation Publishing, 1993), 15.

2 Source: https://americanhistory.si.edu/collections/search/object/nmah_324858.

3 Robert Middlekauff, *The Glorious Cause: The American Revolution: 1763-1789* (New York: Oxford University Press, 2005), 595.

4 Stephen Brumwell, *Redcoats: The British Soldier and War in the Americas, 1755-1763* (New York: Cambridge University Press, 2002), 6.

5 Middlekauff, *The Glorious Cause*, 597.

6 Rick Atkinson, *The British Are Coming: The War for America, Lexington to Princeton, 1775-1777* (New York: Henry Holt & Company, 2019), Kindle, loc. 7112.

7 Ibid., loc. 2869.

8 Ibid., loc. 2849.

9 As quoted in Atkinson, *The British Are Coming*, loc. 2849.

10 William B. Willcox, ed., *The American Rebellion: Sir Henry Clinton's Narrative of His Campaigns, 1775-1782, with an Appendix of Original Documents* (New Haven: Yale University Press, 1954). There are many examples, specifically the 1780 Chesapeake and Carolinas Campaign; see pg. 220.

11 Michael Pearson, *Those Damned Rebels: The American Revolution as Seen Through British Eyes* (Boston: Da Capo Press, 1972), 10.

12 Andrew Jackson O'Shaughnessy, *The Men Who Lost America: British Leadership, the American Revolution, and the Fate of the Empire* (New Haven: Yale University Press, 2013), 355.

13 Source: https://npg.si.edu/object/npg_S_NPG.85.291?destination=edan-search/default_search%3Freturn_all%3D1%26edan_q%3DGeneral%2520Charles%2520Cornwallis%252C%25201st%2520Marquis%2520and%25202nd%2520Earl%2520Cornwallis%252C%2520%26edan_fq%255B0%255D%3Dmedia_usage%253A%2522CC0%2522.

14 John Shy, *A People Numerous and Armed: Reflections on the Military Struggle for American Independence*, Rev. Ed. (Ann Arbor: The University of Michigan Press, 1990), 237.

15 O'Shaughnessy, *The Men Who Lost America*, 355.

16 Ibid., 23.

17 Barbara Tuchman, *The First Salute: A View of the American Revolution* (New York: Ballantine Books, 1988), 149.

18 O'Shaughnessy, *The Men Who Lost America*, 357.

19 Ibid., 56.

20 Atkinson, *The British Are Coming*, Kindle, loc. 3595.

21 Ibid., 121.

22 Shy, *A People Numerous and Armed*, 274.

23 Charles Stedman, *The History of the Origin, Progress, and Termination of the American War in Two Volumes vol.1, 1794* Gale Reprint (New York: Creative Media Partners, 2012), 447.

24 Ibid., 447-448.

25 John S. Pancake, *1777: The Year of the Hangman* (Tuscaloosa, Alabama: The University of Alabama Press, 1977), 226.

26 O'Shaughnessy, *The Men who Lost America*, 353.

27 Ibid., 355.

28 Ibid., 253.

29 bid., 355.

30 Alan Taylor, "Global Revolutions," in the *American Revolution: A World War*, David K. Allison & Larrie D. Ferreiro, Eds. (Washington, DC: Smithsonian Books, 2018), 30.

31 Ibid., 49.

32 Stedman, *The History of the Origin, Progress, and Termination of the American War vol 2*, p 449.

The Doctrines of Imagination: American Foreign Policy & the Images of Puerto Rico, 1898-1965

Carlos A. Santiago
Independent Historian

Abstract

The United States was on the verge of becoming an imperial power in the nineteenth-century. Foreign policy was used as a means to colonize former European outposts like the island of Puerto Rico. While the United States was not powerful enough to enforce foreign policies like the Monroe Doctrine in 1823, it remained hopeful that Europe's power would diminish in Latin America. The Monroe Doctrine had to evolve several times for it to be an effective imperial tool for the United States. The Roosevelt Corollary, the Good Neighbor Policy, and the Truman Doctrine were iterations of the Monroe Doctrine. With each evolution of this foreign policy, the image of Puerto Rico and its people changed along with it. American foreign policy and Puerto Rico are intertwined, which can be seen in the work of American writers from 1898-1965.

Keywords: Monroe Doctrine, Roosevelt Corollary, Good Neighbor Policy, Truman Doctrine, foreign policy, Puerto Rico, imperialism, imperial gaze, American imaginary

Las doctrinas de la imaginación: la política exterior estadounidense y las imágenes de Puerto Rico, 1898-1968

Resumen

Estados Unidos estuvo a punto de convertirse en una potencia imperial en el siglo XIX. La política exterior se utilizó como un medio para colonizar antiguos puestos de avanzada europeos como la isla de Puerto Rico. Si bien Estados Unidos no fue lo suficientemente poderoso para hacer cumplir políticas exteriores como la Doctrina Monroe en 1823, mantuvo la esperanza de que el poder de Europa disminuya en América Latina. La Doctrina Monroe tuvo que evolucionar varias veces para que fuera una herramienta imperial eficaz para Estados Unidos. El Corolario Roosevelt, la Política del Buen Vecino y la Doctrina Truman fueron iteraciones de la Doctrina Monroe. Con cada evolución de esta política exterior, la imagen de Puerto Rico y su gente cambiaba con ella. La política exterior estadounidense y Puerto Rico están entrelazadas, lo que se puede ver en el trabajo de los escritores estadounidenses de 1898-1965.

Palabras clave: Doctrina Monroe, Corolario Roosevelt, Política del Buen Vecino, Doctrina Truman, política exterior, Puerto Rico, imperialismo, mirada imperial, imaginario estadounidense

想象主义：1898-1968年间美国的外交政策和波多黎各的形象

摘要

美国曾在19世纪差点成为一个帝国强国。美国的外交政策曾被用于对当时的欧洲前哨基地（如波多黎各）进行殖民。尽管那时美国的实力还不足以执行像1823年门罗主义这样的外交政策，但其仍然希望欧洲在拉美地区的影响会降低。对美国而言，门罗主义不得不多次发展，以成为一个有效的帝国工具。罗斯福推论、睦邻政策以及杜鲁门主义都是门罗主义的不同演变。随着该外交政策的每一次发展，波多黎各及其人民的形象也随之发生变化。美国的外交政策和波多黎各相互交织，这在1898-1965年间美国作家的作品中有所体现。

关键词：门罗主义，罗斯福推论，睦邻政策，杜鲁门主义，外交政策，波多黎各，帝国主义，帝国的凝视（imperial gaze），美国想象

Introduction

After Florida became a United States territory on March 30th, 1822, President James Monroe was on the verge of making a crucial decision. With Florida no longer in the Spanish Empire's grasp, Monroe's decision had the potential to cement the United States' presence in the Western Hemisphere. Shortly after the end of the American Revolution in 1783, the flames and fervor of rebellion were spreading throughout Latin America and as a result, the Spanish Crown's foothold was waning. This situation presented an opportunity for the United States. After the War of 1812 and decades of being economically dependent on Europe, a weakening Spanish Empire meant that the United States could dream of a future where Europe's interests did not interfere with theirs.

The United States felt Europe's presence often and that set the precedent for the Monroe Doctrine in 1823, which forbade Europe from interfering in the economies of the Western Hemisphere. In the moments leading up to James Monroe's presidency, the United States engaged in "imperial colonialism," which is a term coined by William Appleman Williams to describe the blending of imperialism and anti-colonialism in American nineteenth-century domestic and foreign policy.[1] Moreover, imperial colonialism was a reaction to the United States' own experience with colonialism. Jay Sexton, the author of *The Monroe Doctrine: Empire and Nation in the Nineteenth-Century America*, suggested that in an attempt to "consolidate independence from the British Empire," the United States engaged in "imperial acts" like acquiring new territories and exercising control over Native Americans.[2] The Monroe Doctrine was another reaction to its colonial past.

The implementation of this foreign policy was as bold as it was ambiguous. Although the United States did not have the power to enforce it, the power the Monroe Doctrine would accrue happened over time. The Monroe Doctrine had to evolve as the United States became more powerful. Between 1898 and 1965, the Monroe Doctrine was enforced through extensions like the Roosevelt Corollary, the Good Neighbor Policy, and the Truman Doctrine. Each of these policies affected the island of Puerto Rico.[3]

President Monroe's decision created the paths for the United States and Puerto Rico to cross. Those roads intersected in 1898 and their relationship changed with every evolution of the Monroe Doctrine. The work of American writers between 1898 and 1965 shows that as the United States altered its foreign policy in Latin America, the images of how Americans viewed Puerto Rico and its people changed alongside each shift in foreign policy. Writers such as Howard Grose, Charles H. Rector, Elizabeth and Richard Van Deusen, Ralph Hancock, Ruth Gruber, and Earl Parker Hanson played pivotal roles in describing Puerto Rico over the course of six decades.

From 1898 to 1929, Puerto Rico was seen as a beacon of potential that could be shaped by American economic and cultural ideas of freedom that were antithetical to Spanish colonialism. Puerto Ricans, on the other hand, were viewed as lazy and backwards and who could only be redeemed if they adopted American customs. Between 1930 and 1946, Puerto Rico's image was that of a tropical paradise and Puerto Ricans were praised for their European features. By the Cold War era, Puerto Rico was described as a capitalist economic miracle that was made possible by the United States' resources and Puerto Ricans' hard work and American-like industriousness.

1898-1929: Breaking the Chains of Spanish Colonialism

Puerto Rico and the United States' roads converged during the Spanish-American War of 1898.

Hacienda Aurora, 1898-1899, painted by Francisco Oller. Museo de Arte de Ponce.

The Panic of 1893 economically ravaged the United States. Wounded Knee, Homestead, and tensions between genders and races defined the decade. Diplomatic historian Robert L. Beisner said that the American morale was low enough in the 1890s that the United States needed to "reaffirm American strength: the United States could thrash some other country in a war or, more subtly, demonstrate its ability to govern 'inferior' peoples in an empire."[4] President Theodore Roosevelt, whose life served as a metaphor of masculinity and strength, extended the Monroe Doctrine through the Roosevelt Corollary to make governing a Latin American territory possible with the United States serving as a massive guard with a gun.[5] The United States needed its morale to be boosted after several years of economic calamity. A war and claiming lands were looked at as remedies for this problem.

When the Spanish-American War ended, the territories that the United States acquired from Spain consisted of Guam, the Philippine islands and Puerto Rico. Because of the United States' experience as a colony, Americans were not fond of imperialism. The country did not even consider itself an imperial power after claiming land from Spain. Instead, the United States justified its newfound powerful presence in Latin America as an action that would cause Europe's foothold in the region to dwindle. The language used to justify the acquisition of oversea territories hailed the United States as a helpful and beneficial force that could instill economic and governmental freedom to its neighbors. For the United States, freedom was the answer and colonialism was a relic of the past.

The Organic Act of 1900 in Puerto Rico is an example of the United States justifying its imperial pursuits. Once it was enacted, Puerto Rico gained a representative House of Delegates that ensured there was an American majority in the house and an American-appointed governor.⁶ This hypocritical action was justified because the United States communicated that this law would help civilize Puerto Rico, develop its economy, and undo Puerto Rico's past Spanish colonial ties. Puerto Rico was receiving a lesson on freedom.

American writers echoed the sentiments of legislation like the Organic Act as they described Puerto Rico and its people. These descriptions created images of Puerto Rico and Puerto Ricans. In this case, members of the Young People's Missionary Movement of the United States, an organization of evangelical Christian missionaries, had the goal of civilizing and bringing God's prosperity to Puerto Rico.⁷ One of the organization's leaders, Howard Grose wrote a book in 1909 titled *Aliens or Americans?* where he points to four problems that plagued Puerto Rico. The first two problems were the tyranny of the Spanish empire and "the economic oppression of the people." The Catholic Church and the lack of education across the island were the following two problems. In essence, every problem that Grose noted was linked to the Spanish and their imperial practices. Spanish imperialism held Puerto Rico back from being self-dependent, according to Grose and he deduced that Puerto Rico had the potential to become an economically prosperous island with an American helping hand that was not neglectful like Spain.⁸

Similar to Grose, an author named Charles H. Rector wrote a book in 1898 about Puerto Rico titled, *The Story of Beautiful Puerto Rico: Graphic Description of the Garden Spot of the World by Pen and Camera*, which evaluated the island's economic potential. Topics included discussions on the land, the Puerto Rican people, and what ailed the island. He found that Puerto Rico's reliance on cash crops like tobacco, sugar, and coffee were crucial to the Puerto Rican economy. Before American occupation, Puerto Rico was hurt economically by high Spanish tariffs. Puerto Rican coffee and tobacco were not of better quality than its Brazilian and Cuban counterparts. Sugar cultivation was an industry in decline. Puerto Rico focused on the production of cane sugar while other parts of the Caribbean cultivated beet sugar. Cane sugar yielded less than beet sugar and was more difficult to produce. With slavery abolished in Puerto Rico in 1873, there was no modern industrial infrastructure that could possibly help produce the same output as enslaved people were producing prior to 1873.⁹ Rector believed that with the help of the United States, Puerto Rico could obtain the infrastructure needed to increase production. He believed that with US intervention Puerto Rico had the potential to double the sugar it exported.¹⁰ Rector's comments highlighted that Puerto Rico could improve with the United States' guidance. Puerto Ricans were viewed with similar promise despite their negative portrayal.

Puerto Ricans were largely viewed as exotic, backwards, and lazy in this period. Although Americans saw Puerto Ricans in that light, they thought the United States could redeem them. Rector thought that if Puerto

Ricans were introduced to American ways, they could become good workers. He believed Puerto Ricans to be lazy and his diagnosis was that laziness was linked to Spanish colonialism, which kept Puerto Ricans "in debt."[11] The United States appeared to have a prescription for Puerto Rico's economic problems so that it could attain economic freedom.

Since the Spanish had their own subjects in debt, Rector felt the island lacked "some of the qualities of the stalwart American type." And this condition consisted of the "impossibility" of ordinary Puerto Ricans having a say in their government. Their limitedness, as Rector described it, was the reason why Puerto Ricans were lazy, which was a characteristic that he was sure would be eradicated if the United States lent a hand to Puerto Rico so that they may "rise by the work of their hand." An alliance between Puerto Rico and the United States could allow the island to spur "into greater and remunerative activity."[12]

Puerto Ricans were expected to adopt American economic customs as well as American culture. Elizabeth and Richard Van Deusen published a children's short story in 1927 that implied that Puerto Ricans could engage with American traditions. "Porto Rican Snow" was a story that focused on the experience of two boys named William and Ricardo. William was from the United States and Ricardo was Puerto Rican. In the story, Ricardo notices that William was upset and asks him what was wrong. William said he was homesick; a feeling that had been intensifying because he could not fathom Christmas being two weeks away with no snowy hills to go sledding to make him cherish the holiday season. Ricardo tried to cheer him up and asked him to accompany him and his father to see the snow on the mountain towns of "Aibonito or Adjuntas." Curious to see if Ricardo was bluffing, William joined Ricardo and his father on the trip and grew pleasantly surprised. Not only was the weather brisk, but Ricardo's father pointed towards some white matter towards the side of a mountain that had William ecstatic. "Snow! Snow! Snow!" William exclaimed. He even became euphoric once he got to go sledding down a hill.[13]

What William believed to be snow was not snow. The white matter on the mountains were white tarps that covered tobacco plants from getting scorched by the sun. William wanted to experience an American Christmas that he was familiar with, which is what Ricardo and his father helped him experience. This story holds Christmas as an American tradition. In Puerto Rico, Christmas Day is celebrated as it is in many other parts of the Christian world. However, Puerto Ricans hold early January's Three Kings Day as the pinnacle of the Christmas season. Therefore, "Porto Rican Snow" is not a short story about a boy who misses snow. It is a short story of a practice and holiday that Puerto Ricans can adopt alongside Three Kings Day to make them more American.

1930-1946: Repairing the Image of Puerto Ricans

Three years after the publication of "Porto Rican Snow," the world economy crashed and the Great Depression ensued. After 1929, the United States shifted its foreign policy in Latin America. The image of Puerto Rico and its people in the American imagination changed as well. The next evolution of the Monroe Doctrine began during Franklin D. Roosevelt's administration in the 1930s. The Good Neighbor Policy became the successor to the Roosevelt Corollary. In an effort to foster relationships in Latin America during World War II, FDR used the Good Neighbor Policy to tackle the misconceptions of Latin America in the minds of Americans. FDR promised to stop intervening in Latin American countries while extending them respect, equality, and fraternity.[14] To do that, the images of the United States' Latin American neighbors needed to be repaired after decades of damage.

Puerto Rico's image was repaired through this initiative. The island was described as a tropical paradise because of its physical features and Puerto Ricans were embraced for their white features. With the demand of cane sugar dropping precipitously during the Great Depression, the Puerto Rican economy sought to find another way to sustain itself. To do so, the economy looked to emulate other Caribbean islands like Cuba and Jamaica that had adopted tourism with fantastic results.[15]

Discover Puerto Rico U.S.A. Where the Americas Meet, painted by Frank S. Nicholson. NYC Art Project, WPA.

Soon, writers like Richard Van Deusen continued to play a role in creating images of Puerto Rico through their descriptions. In 1931, Van Deusen wrote *Puerto Rico: A Caribbean Isle*, which is a book that emphasized that Puerto Rico was "not merely material riches, but embraces the idea of luxuriousness, of lavish beauty, of deep contentment, of slumberous peace, of constant pleasure and plentiful harvests…"[16] Describing Puerto Rico as a place that is not materialistically rich is significant because he wrote of Puerto Rico's natural beauties as a commodity that can be sold. Puerto Rico's prior image of being a land of problems was changing as some misconceptions of the island were addressed through the Good Neighbor Policy. The demand for travel guides rose as Puerto Rico became known for its "legend, romance, scenic beauty and cultural traditions" rather than the backwardness it was attributed to years prior.[17]

Van Deusen's description of Puerto Rico is appealing to Americans because beauty became a commodity that could be sold. As the island was depicted as a tropical paradise, the image of the Puerto Rico was no longer associated with laziness and backwardness. The repairs made to the image of Puerto Rico itself meant that the misconceptions of Puerto Ricans needed to be addressed too. FDR's Good Neighbor Policy led to Puerto Ricans becoming recognized for their ethnic whiteness and their willingness to become Americans rather than their blackness.

Van Deusen addressed the misconception that it "is sometimes erroneously stated that Puerto Rico is a country of negroes."[18] In 1920, Puerto Rico's population was 73 percent white, 23.3 percent mulatto, and 3.8 percent black. Van Deusen thought that since white people overwhelmingly outnumbered black people it meant that the black population would eventually "fall into insignificance."[19]

He described Puerto Rico in the sixteen-century as a military colony that encouraged a great influx of population through the "constant renewal of the garrison." The Puerto Rican population was infused with "Flemish, Walloons, Alsatians, Poles, and Italians" people that were historically and ethnologically merged with the Spanish "leaving but their foreign names."[20] Along with those peoples, Frenchmen and Spanish Dominicans made their way to the neighboring island as well. Since the island had a substantial population of Europeans breeding with Puerto Ricans, the people on the island were not just attaining European traditions, but they were also "whitening."[21] And it is because of this sense of whiteness that Americans believed Puerto Ricans could become Americans themselves. Van Deusen was aware of how difficult it would be to Americanize Puerto Ricans, but he was convinced that the traditions that they had obtained through European immigration would encourage them to adopt American traditions.

Van Deusen saw potential in them due to their "qualities of hidaligoism," which is a Spanish term referring to word "gentleman." Those qualities consist of "honor, gallantry, dignity" and "pride." These characteristics were "all deeply ingrained in the character of the Porto Rican."[22] Van Deusen also said he admired the people's "family devotion." The Puerto Rican familial relationship was one Van Deusen regarded as one based on respect and sharing. What he found most admirable was that Puerto Ricans possessed "a superior intelligence with ability to grasp an idea readily."[23] What Van Deusen was saying was different from what Puerto Ricans were described as earlier in the century. He depicted them as people who were different due to their Latin traditions and cultures while making it clear that Puerto Ricans could become Americans because of their qualities. The Good Neighbor Policy seemed to have worked for Puerto Rico's image. What was to come next was a Puerto Rico that was praised during the Cold War.

1946-1965: Puerto Rico is a Capitalist Miracle

Operation Bootstrap, which took place between 1947 and 1960, was a program that transformed the Puerto Rican economy.[24] With the help of the Puerto Rico Industrial Development Company and the United States federal government, Operation Bootstrap's projects became known for leading to the increase in manufacturing, export production and the quality of life of Puerto Ricans.[25] By 1947, the Truman Doctrine marked the beginning of the Cold War, which was an extension of the Monroe Doctrine that sought to ward off communism in the Western Hemisphere. Under this condition, the United States and American writers fabricated an image of Puerto Rico that served as proof to the world that capitalism worked more effectively than communism. Puerto Ricans' image also improved, for they could have their own George Washington-esque figure for them to follow.

Cold War sentiments viewed Puerto Rico as a capitalist success story that otherwise would not have been possible if it were not for the United States' help and the efforts of hard-working Puerto Ricans. Once viewed as a disease-ridden, overpopulated and underdeveloped island, Puerto Rico now stood "as a prosperous, healthy land of opportunity."[26]

Puerto Rico: A Success Story by Ralph Hancock was a book published in 1960 that hailed the United States as a friendly capitalist force that helped Puerto Rico become a success. Capitalism and communism were competing on a global scale triggering the discourse and critiques of both systems. With that said, Hancock would go on to state that capitalism was not "synonymous with aggression" but progress. And Puerto Rico served as a shining example of United States' "benevolent" interests and living proof that both parties can work together in harmony.[27]

Puerto Rico: Island of Promise, also published in 1960, has author Ruth Gruber pose that Puerto Rico was going in the right direction due to American economic intervention. She said that before United States intervention in Puerto Rico there was "beauty and wealth in a few sections, and poverty and hunger nearly everywhere else."²⁸ She described slums throughout the island as "shocking hell-holes" and mentioned that they were decreasing in size due to the help of the United States. Growth within the middle class also encouraged Gruber to describe 1960s Puerto Rico as a place that was undergoing a capitalist "revolution."²⁹

Earl Parker Hanson, one of Gruber's contemporaries, echoed her sentiments. Hanson's *Transformation: The Story of Modern Puerto Rico* was published in 1955 and it praised Puerto Rico's capitalist transformation. In the book, Hanson believed that capitalism increased the "human energies" of the Puerto Ricans. In his eyes this led to Puerto Ricans increasing their attempts to remedy problems that plagued the island. The person who would go on to encapsulate the very essence of "human energies" would be Luis Muñoz Marin. This man was not just Puerto Rico's first democratically elected governor, but he was also the prime depiction of how a Puerto Rican could be considered a model American.³⁰

Marin had become so venerated among Americans and Puerto Ricans that he was given the moniker, the "George Washington of Puerto Rico."³¹ Being revered as something close to a deity—as George Washington is oftentimes considered throughout American history—Marin became the epitome of an American gentleman. According to Ralph Hancock, Marin not only studied, but he attended the prestigious Georgetown University, and had a successful career as a poet.

One of Marin's poems that Hancock really enjoyed, states:

> I have broken the rainbow
>
> Against my heart
>
> As one breaks a useless sword against a knee.
>
> I have blown the clouds of rose color and blood color beyond the farthest horizons.
>
> I have drowned my dreams
>
> In order to glut the dreams that sleep for me in the veins of men who sweated and wept and raged
>
> To season my coffee…³²

Hancock believed that this poem "articulates feelings" Marin "had for the complex social problems of Puerto Rico."³³ Hancock was by no means wrong. Marin was known for adopting American commercial practices to grow the market of Puerto Rico in hopes of lessening poverty on the island. Between the 1940s and 1960s, suburbs began to be developed, slums were subsisting, "highways networks" were being paved, and megastores made their ways into "most old town centers."³⁴

The capitalist revolution that Americans believed was occurring in Puerto Rico was precisely what the Truman Doctrine tried to achieve in the region. Puerto Rico served as an example for Americans to use to articulate that capitalism was more effective than communism. Puerto Rico and Puerto Rican's image improved as a result.

Conclusion

The history that the United States and Puerto Rico share began with James Monroe who became the architect of the United States' imperialism overseas through the Monroe Doctrine. This doctrine became a playbook that subsequent presidents and officials used and strengthened depending on the context. The products of those efforts to strengthen the foreign policy introduced by the Monroe Doctrine affected Puerto Rico. They came in the form of the Roosevelt Corollary, the Good Neighbors Policy, and the Truman Doctrine. American writers were enamored with the world and the place their country played in it. Their writing is what allows us to see how the United States viewed Puerto Rico and its people across time. Their work and the analysis of their work provide us with a blueprint to observe and identify the images of Puerto Rico and its people in any era, whether it is in the past or in the future.

Bibliography

Ayala, Cesar J, & Rafael Bernabe. *Puerto Rico in the American Century: A History Since 1898*. Chapel Hill: The University of North Carolina Press, 2007.

Combs, Jerald A. *The History of American Foreign Policy from 1895*, 4th ed. New York: Taylor & Francis, 2015.

Grose, Howard B. *Advance in the Antilles: The New Era in Cuba and Porto Rico*. Philadelphia: The American Baptist Publication Society, 1910.

Grose, Howard B. *Aliens or Americans?* New York: Young People's Missionary Movement of the United States and Canada, 1909.

Gruber, Ruth. *Puerto Rico: Island of Promise*. New York: Hill and Wang, 1960.

Hancock, Ralph. *Puerto Rico: A Success Story*. Princeton: Van Nostrand, 1960.

Hanson, Earl P. *Transformation: The Story of Modern Puerto Rico*. New York: Alfred A. Knopf, Inc., 1955.

Perez Jr., Louis A. *The War of 1898: The United States and Cuba in History and Historiography*. Chapel Hill: University of North Carolina Press, 1998.

Rector, Charles H. *The Story of Beautiful Porto Rico: A Graphic Description of the Garden Spot of the World by Pen and Camera*. London: Forgotten Books, 2015.

Rosas, Richard. "Business as Pleasure: Culture, Tourism and Nation in Puerto Rico in the 1930's." *Nepantla: Views from South* 2, no. 3 (2001): 453.

Sexton, Jay. *The Monroe Doctrine: Empire and Nation in the Nineteenth-Century America*. New York: Hill and Wang, 2011.

Stuckey, Mary E. *The Good Neighbor: Franklin D. Roosevelt and the Rhetoric of American Power*. East Lansing: Michigan State University Press, 2013.

Van Deusen, Elizabeth Kniepple. *Stories of Porto Rico*. San Juan: Department of Education, 1927.

Van Deusen, Richard J. *Porto Rico: A Caribbean Isle*. New York: Henry Holt & Company, Inc, 1931.

Notes

1. Jay Sexton, *Monroe Doctrine: Empire and Nation in the Nineteenth-Century America* (New York: Hill and Wang, 2011), 6.

2. Ibid.

3. Ibid., 3.

4. Louis A. Perez Jr., *The War of 1898: The United States and Cuba in History and Historiography* (Chapel Hill: University of North Carolina Press, 1998), 1-3.

5. Ibid.

6. Jerald A. Combs, *The History of American Foreign Policy from 1895*, 4th ed. (New York: Taylor & Francis, 2015), chap. 3, Kindle.

7. Howard B. Grose, *Advance in the Antilles: The New Era in Cuba and Porto Rico* (Philadelphia: The American Baptist Publication Society, 1910), 10-12.

8. Howard B. Grose, *Aliens or Americans?* (New York: Young People's Missionary Movement of the United States and Canada, 1909), 15.

9. Richard Rosas, "Business as Pleasure: Culture, Tourism and Nation in Puerto Rico in the 1930's," *Nepantla: Views from South* 2, no. 3, (2001): 453.

10. Charles H. Rector, *The Story of Beautiful Porto Rico: A Graphic Description of the Garden Spot of the World by Pen and Camera* (London: Forgotten Books, 2015), 13.

11. Ibid., 125.

12. Ibid., 50.

13 Elizabeth & Richard Van Deusen, *Stories of Porto Rico* (San Juan: Department of Education, 1927), 1-8.

14 Mary E. Stuckey, *The Good Neighbor: Franklin D. Roosevelt and the Rhetoric of American Power* (East Lansing: Michigan State University Press, 2013), 173-174.

15 Rosas, "Business as Pleasure," 450.

16 Richard J. Van Deusen, *Porto Rico: A Caribbean Isle* (New York: Henry Holt & Company, Inc, 1931), 1-7.

17 Ibid., 1.

18 Ibid., 158.

19 Ibid.

20 Ibid., 159.

21 Ibid.

22 Ibid., 158-162.

23 Ibid., 163

24 Cesar J. Ayala & Rafael Bernabe, *Puerto Rico in the American Century: A History Since 1898* (Chapel Hill, The University of North Carolina Press, 2007), 180.

25 Ibid., 183.

26 Ralph Hancock, *Puerto Rico: A Success Story* (Princeton: Van Nostrand, 1960), 1.

27 Ibid., 3.

28 Ruth Gruber, *Puerto Rico: Island of Promise* (New York: Hill and Wang, 1960), 8.

29 Ibid.

30 Earl P. Hanson, *Transformation: The Story of Modern Puerto Rico* (New York: Alfred A. Knopf, Inc., 1955), 5.

31 Hancock, *Puerto Rico*, 77.

32 Ibid., 5.

33 Ibid., 6.

34 Ayala and Bernabe, *Puerto Rico in the American Century*, 201-202.

A Division At War—Part II

Dr. Robert Young
Associate Professor, Department of History and Military History
American Military University

Abstract

During World War II, the U.S. 32nd Infantry Division fought a long line of vicious battles in the Southwest Pacific Area, primarily on the island of New Guinea and in the Philippines. New Guinea was frustrating and costly. The Philippines took it to a whole other level. On Leyte, the 32nd entered after the operation began and though costly it was perhaps their easiest campaign of the war. From Leyte they moved to the main Philippine island of Luzon, where the Division would toil throughout the spring of 1945. The Villa Verde Trail on Luzon became the name synonymous with the 32nd Infantry Division in World War II. They fought with honor and distinction despite achieving little. Such was the nature of the war on Luzon in 1945.

Keywords: 32nd Infantry Division, Leyte-Luzon-Philippines-World War II, U.S. Sixth Army

Una división en guerra—Parte II

Resumen

Durante la Segunda Guerra Mundial, la 32.a División de Infantería de EE. UU. Libró una larga serie de feroces batallas en el área del Pacífico suroeste, principalmente en la isla de Nueva Guinea y Filipinas. Nueva Guinea era frustrante y costosa. Filipinas lo llevó a otro nivel. En Leyte, el 32 entró después de que comenzara la operación y, aunque costosa, fue quizás la campaña más fácil de la guerra. De Leyte se trasladaron a la principal isla filipina de Luzón, donde la División trabajaría duro durante la primavera de 1945. El Camino de Villa Verde en Luzón se convirtió en el nombre sinónimo de la 32ª División de Infantería en la Segunda Guerra Mundial. Lucharon con honor y distinción a pesar de lograr poco. Tal fue la naturaleza de la guerra de Luzón en 1945.

Palabras clave: 32a División de Infantería, Leyte-Luzón-Filipinas-Segunda Guerra Mundial, Sexto Ejército de EE. UU.

战争中的一个师—第二部分

摘要

二战期间,美国陆军第32步兵师在西南太平洋地区进行了一连串艰苦战斗,战斗集中在新几内亚岛和菲律宾。新几内亚的战斗是令人沮丧和代价巨大的。菲律宾的战斗则上升到完全的新高度。第32步兵师在战斗打响后进入莱特岛,尽管损失巨大,但这场战役可能是最容易的一场战斗。莱特岛战役结束后他们转向菲律宾主岛吕宋岛,并在那里艰难度过了1945年春季。吕宋岛上的维拉维德步道(Villa Verde Trail)成为了二战时期第32步兵师的同义词。尽管取得的战果甚微,但第32步兵师的战斗是荣誉和卓越的。这便是1945年吕宋岛战役的性质。

关键词:美国陆军第32步兵师,莱特岛-吕宋岛-菲律宾-二战,美国第六军团

Of the many infantry divisions that had the honor and at the same time misfortune to fight in the Southwest Pacific Area (SWPA) during World War II, the 32nd Infantry Division (ID) stands at the top. The top, in this case, is not a place of distinction. The 32nd deserves all the kudos possible for their record in New Guinea (the subject of Part I in my series on this division) and as will become obvious in the coming pages for their struggles in the Philippines. Here, the top is reserved for the unit given one impossible mission after the other in the worst possible terrain, understrength, and devoid of support from higher commands. It began on New Guinea with Buna in 1942, and along the Driniumor River in 1944. As the SWPA moved to the Philippines, the 32nd ID once again played a prominent role. On Leyte, the first major operation of the Philippines campaign, the 32nd entered the fray several weeks after its initiation. On Luzon, all the division had previously experienced paled in comparison. The Villa Verde Trail became the symbol of a heroic unit's struggle in World War II.

When Leyte began, the 32nd ID was in the vicinity of the island of Samar. They arrived on Leyte in mid-November 1944. Initially, missions included relieving units recently victorious, such as the 21st Infantry Regiment on Breakneck Ridge, mopping up isolated Japanese detachments, and attacking specific positions such as "Corkscrew Ridge," a series of hills that took several weeks to clear.[1] They would then head south and spend most of the remaining campaign in the Ormoc Valley, along

Highway 2. By the middle of December, after heavy fighting, the 32nd breached the main Japanese defensive line. Through the end of December, the division drove west against light resistance. Though the 32nd saw heavy action only sporadically on Leyte, the cost was still high: 450 dead and 1,491 wounded.[2] Those losses were not replaced before the move to Luzon. Making matters worse, the losses suffered in the Driniumor River fight on New Guinea only a few months earlier were also still not replaced. The division had suffered similar casualties, in numbers (450 dead, 1,500 wounded), at the Driniumor as it did on Leyte.[3] 4,000 men lost, none replaced. Those that remained were tired when departing for Luzon.

In no way am I trying to dismiss the 32nd Infantry Division's struggles on Leyte. It is just completely overshadowed by what they experienced on Luzon. On Luzon, it came down to four words—the Villa Verde Trail. John Carlisle, in *Red Arrow Men: Stories About the 32nd Division on the Villa Verde Trail*, states what the division faced along that trail:

> This was a mauling fight against the Jap in his remarkable defensive positions, against the terrain, supply, and climate. In those 119 days, the Red Arrow boys fought 22 miles, sometimes 35 yards at a time, with the Japanese never more than 30 feet away. The division killed 9,000 Japs and took 50 prisoners. It lost 4,226 men, about a third of the division strength.[4]

The fight will be addressed in the coming pages. First, was this fight even necessary? A vigorous strategic debate preceded General Douglas MacArthur's "Return to the Philippines" should all resources be devoted to Admiral Chester Nimitz's Central Pacific drive, or to MacArthur's quest to reclaim lost territory, specifically the Philippines. That debate is beyond this article's scope.[5] It did undoubtedly make many wonder why they fought on these islands. Was it for MacArthur's ego? Move forward to the fight for Luzon itself. Once the decision to retake the vast archipelago was made, Luzon, as the largest island and home to Manila, its largest port and prominent air bases and lodgment areas for a future invasion of Japan, was the obvious main target. The U.S. Sixth Army, under the command of General Walter Krueger, invaded Luzon in January 1945. By the end of February Manila and all points south were either secure or being secured. The Japanese army on Luzon was still formidable, over 150,000 men, most of them on the northern part of the island. They were formidable in numbers, not capability. They had no air cover, no transport. The American forces around Manila were under no threat from the Japanese—a token defensive or covering force was all that was needed. To make these Japanese forces relevant American units had to attack them, in strong defensive positions the enemy prepared for over three years. Of course, American forces attacked. The Sixth Army noted this in their history of the campaign, stating:

> ... by making us come into the mountain, after him, he hoped to

meet us on ground of his choosing, afflict maximum casualties, and compel us to maintain a large force in northern Luzon for a long time to come, thus correspondingly reducing the forces which we would have available for operations elsewhere.[6]

General MacArthur wanted all Japanese forces destroyed. Therefore, General Krueger wanted them destroyed. He tasked his I Corps, with the 25th, 32nd, and 33rd Infantry Divisions, with destroying the Japanese forces to their north. The 25th fought for the Balete Pass. The 33rd drove towards the town of Baguio. The 32nd would slug it out along the Villa Verde Trail.

Villa Verde Trail is not a misnomer. That's all it was, a trail. The Japanese 2nd Tank Division (with no tanks) defended it. The veterans of the Division noted:

> The terrain in this area was much worse than any that the Division had so far encountered. Hills with nearly perpendicular slopes and deep, precipitous ravines made all movements exceedingly difficult. The enemy had, moreover, utilized the terrain to best advantage by constructing numerous mutually supporting cave positions, which had to be reduced one by one, in order to permit the eastward advance of the Division to continue. The advance was, moreover, flanked 1,500-2,000 yards north of and parallel to the Villa Verde Trail by Mt. Imugan, on the forward slopes of which the enemy had established defensive positions and artillery observation posts. The Mt. Imugan positions dominated a stretch of over two miles of the Villa Verde Trail and his observation stations enabled the enemy to adjust his artillery fire on troops and vehicles moving along the trail, which ran along the crest of razor back ridges and formed the only route of advance. Besides, the Mt. Imugan positions enabled the enemy to repulse any direct attack through the valley north of the trail and constituted an ever-present threat to the line of communications of the 32nd Division. Under the circumstances, with the enemy holding Mt. Imugan, the 32nd Division had no choice but to crack the enemy defenses on the dominating hills directly in its front some four miles west of Imugan village, since bypassing them was not possible. The resulting struggle was slow and bloody and demanded the utmost of valor and fortitude on the part of our troops, especially since the division was unable to bring all its power into play, because it had to protect its rearward communications all the way from its front lines to Saint Nicolas.[7]

The main portion of the 32nd's fight took place along less than a six-mile stretch, the distance between the start point, Santa Maria, and the ultimate objective, Santa Fe. They never made it to Santa

Fe. Getting into position alone took nearly a month of heavy fighting. The losses incurred in that move exacerbated an already dangerous personnel situation. The 32nd entered Luzon with only 11,000 officers and men, 4,000 below their authorized strength (those 4,000 were the losses in the Driniumor River and Leyte campaigns[8]). Due to all the operations going on throughout the SWPA and on different parts of Luzon, no reinforcements or additional support were available.

Lack of men alone did not plague the 32nd. The terrain was so miserable that an effective supply route did not exist. The division had to build one as it moved, all under Japanese observation and machine gun, mortar, and artillery fire. General William Gill, the division commander, noted:

> ... the 32nd Division was headed for the Villa Verde Trail, which was nothing more or less than a foot trail over the mountains. As far as our 32nd Division was concerned, our first job was to build some kind of a road ... We had to supply ourselves with food and water, and while the road was being built[,] we were fighting at the same time ... General Krueger came up to see me quite often on the Villa Verde Trail (once we got road enough for a jeep to come up) and he says in his book of having made several personnel inspections, that his conclusion very definitely was that it would be a long, slow, and costly operation. And indeed that's what it turned out to be. Morale was poor because the men were tired. They had been in there in combat for months, they had had only a little rest after Leyte and during January, February, March, and April we had to fight the Japs on the trail and build the road at the same time.[9]

Tank support was unavailable because of the terrain. Artillery and air support were discarded because of poor observation and the close proximity of Japanese and American forces. It was a small-unit infantry fight on numbered hills and the Salacsac Passes. To progress, the 32nd had to get through those passes. To get to the passes they first had to move up the Trail under the continual observation of the Japanese from those endless hills.

The 32nd's fight happened in two phases. The first, between March and mid-April, was little more than a stalemate in the vicinity of Salacsac Pass #2. The second phase continued until the division was finally pulled off the line at the end of May, with the fighting moving toward Salacsac Pass #1. I Corps noted in its history of the campaign what the 32nd faced in its first days on the Trail:

> Fiercest enemy resistance continued to be met along the VILLA VERDE TRAIL west of IMUGAN where the Japanese were taking full advantage of high ground studded with mutually supporting pillboxes and caves. Routes of advance offered only sparse cover, making concealed maneuver virtually impossible.[10]

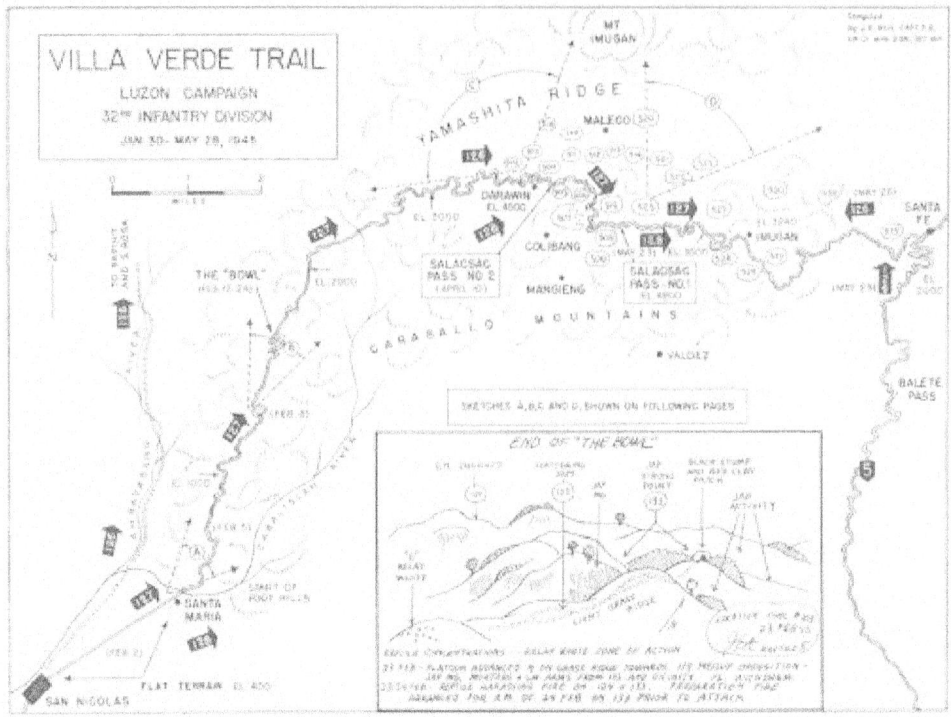

A division rendering of the Trail, the positions occupied by the Japanese, and the dominating high ground.[11]

An actual view of the Villa Verde Trail and the dominating high ground.[12]

It would take the 127th Infantry Regiment (along with the 126th and 128th, the three divisional infantry regiments) two weeks to advance only 1,000 yards from Hill 502 to Hill 505. Two weeks! There was plentiful air (two squadrons—32 planes—of P-51 Mustang fighter bombers) and artillery support (12 guns). The jungle made the bombing and artillery fire very inaccurate, it could never be observed and adjusted. Inaccurate maps further denigrated artillery fire and replacements would take several weeks to arrive. Nothing seemed to be working.[13] The fight then fell to the infantry. The bombing and artillery blew jungle all over the place and even further camouflaged Japanese positions. The hills were steep and strewn with caves. One would be dealt with and several more popped up, often to the rear of an advance. The frustration felt by the ground troops and the task facing them is clear in the Division's AAR:

> The movements of Co. C for the next two days best understand the laborious and costly process of reducing the cave position. Troops of this company found, after several failures, that to reduce the cave system it was necessary to attack two or more positions simultaneously while keeping those on the flanks neutralized by machine gun and mortar fire. In this manner two platoons inched their way from the top of Hill 502 down two noses, which were supported by a ravine. These two platoons provided cross-supporting fire for each other, while the heavy weapons company from positions at the bottom of the hill, protected the flanks. Once on top of the caves, various methods were used to deal with the occupants. Smoke grenades, when thrown into an entrance revealed that the caves were connected by tunnels, since smoke would often come out of another hole some distance away. This led our troops to seal the entrances by caving in the ceiling with demolitions and by piling soil in front from above. Jap reactions to this tactic provided some uneasy moments to our troops. After sealing the caves during the day, our troops were kept awake during the night by the muffled sounds of the Japs trying to dig their way to the surface of the ground in the middle of the company perimeter.[14]

Once Hill 502 was COMPLETELY secure the unit moved on and the same process began again on the next hill.

The 32nd was an experienced combat organization. They fought in the jungle of Buna, along the Driniumor River, and at Leyte. This took it to another degree of difficulty and frustration. The Trail could not support tanks or heavy equipment. The road being built could not reach the front line. In these early weeks the 127th IR did most of the fighting. The regiment had an authorized strength of 3,200 men but entered this battle with only 2,100. By the end of March, it suffered 110 killed, 225 wounded, and 500 non-battle casualties, nearly half their remaining strength. Non-battle casualties suffered from heat exhaustion, sickness, and combat fatigue. The Regimental medical assets could not hope to deal with this massive number of non-battle casualties. No psychologists were available and all the 127th's Regimental Surgeon seemed to get was exasperation from commanders that so many were sick. Any concerns for the problem were ignored, the Surgeon noting: "As usual however, no suggestion on how to combat these problems were forthcoming, nor was any credence placed in the explanation of the medical officers immediately concerned with the problem."[15] The 127th was mercifully pulled off the line. The 126th and 128th Infantry Regiments fared little better.[16]

Reinforcements were needed. General Gill asked his immediate superior, I Corps Commander General Innis Swift, for help. Swift's answer was straightforward and simple: "…there were no reinforcements available either in the Corps or in General Krueger's army."[17] General Gill was infuriated by this situation and the unrealistic expectations heaped upon his men to accomplish their mission as understrength as the 32nd was, noting:

> It's all well and good to sit back and say that (accomplish the mission without reinforcements) … But there are casualties other than battle casualties, particularly after a long period of hard fighting and exposure to the elements, to the diseases and all the things that go to reduce the capabilities of fighting men. For example, we had all sorts of dysentery and malaria cases, the weather was bad … Those things contributed a great deal to the lessening of our fighting abilities.[18]

The 32nd did receive replacements as the battle progressed, 238 officers and 6,661 enlisted men, a seemingly impressive number. Those men did not come in bulk and a replacement needs time to be integrated into a unit, especially a green, recent graduate of basic training. That is difficult under normal circumstances, in combat it is foolhardy. 214 officers and 5,747 enlisted men also returned throughout the campaign from the hospital. They were far from stellar upon their return. The Division's AAR even stated these returning men "…should be assigned directly to some service installations." Between replacements and returning troops you had nearly 13,000 men yet the Division never approached full strength. Losses, especially non-battle casualties, exceeded any returning men.[19]

For the campaign to progress Salacsac Pass #2, the ravine between Hills 504 and 505, had to be taken. After Hill 504 was finally secured the 128th IR attacked Hill 505. Defended by approximately 1,800 Japanese soldiers it mattered little how much American firepower hit that hill. Every attack was thrown back. Caves and bunkers just gave the defenders too much of an advantage. Assault teams with their bazookas, demolitions, and flamethrowers could never get close enough to finish the Japanese off. In an action reminiscent of Washington's army digging trenches towards Cornwallis at Yorktown during the Revolutionary War, an entire battalion of the 128th IR dug trenches to within a few feet of the caves. Caves were blasted and sealed.[20] This action was typical of the entire campaign: prolonged attacks against single positions. Hill 505, one hill, took a month to secure. That hill exacted enough of a toll that the 128th had to be pulled off the line for a rest. The 126th remained in the fight, the 127th would soon return. Torrential rains then added more misery to the infantryman's daily life.

The 127th returned seemingly, according to the Regiment's AAR, ready to fight and with high morale. That was the 18th of April. By the 21st, three days later, reality sunk in once again. Many criticized Japanese doctrine because of their defensive mindset; it is far easier to destroy an enemy in the open. Yet, a returning member of the 127th noted: "… that whenever we take up position now, the Japanese have a better one. They are emplaced on all the really strategic high hills and mountains. It is impossible to locate their artillery, mortar or machine gun emplacements. They are masters of camouflage."[21] Psycho-neurotic cases rose, exhaustion was everywhere. To get to Salacsac Pass #1, Hill 508, one half of the Pass' anchor, had to be taken. Phase 2 of the campaign began.

The 127th IR continually attacked Hill 508 and as with other battles accomplished little. Hill 508 was not the only problem. Neighboring Hill 507 also poured fire onto the 127th. That occurred continuously along the Villa Verde Trail, Japanese fire from neighboring hills harassing American troops while attacking one specific hill. Hill 507 had 65 Japanese caves that were sealed but other Japanese positions continued to harass other American units on that hill and Hill 508. Nothing ever seemed to be truly secure. Until the end of May the 127th would seal off the incredible number of 500 caves on these hills. Each cave required an assault team and hard, dangerous work. The 127th was finished as a combat unit by the end of this fight.[22]

Hill 526, the other anchor of Salacsac Pass #1, was the new mission for the returning 128th IR. It would take until 10 May to finally secure it. Yamashita Ridge became the objective; its heights dominated the entire area. Several different hills had to be taken first and a crude supply trail, frequently cut by the Japanese, was far from reliable. The 128th, with help from the 126th, took the rest of the month to secure Salacsac Pass #1. Mercifully, the 32nd ID was finally pulled off the line on 31 May.

Luzon and the Villa Verde Trail took a frightful toll on an already tired infantry division. 916 killed, 2,500 wounded, and 5,00 non-battle casualties (just the ones reported, the number is probably far higher).[23] They accomplished their mission but at what long-term cost? Psychological and non-battle casualties were not a prominent issue in this era of the U.S. military. It certainly existed; it just was not acknowledged. The term Post Traumatic Stress Disorder (PTSD) at that time didn't even exist. The Division records don't offer much help dissecting the problem of non-battle casualties. If not for the 127th IR's Surgeon, little would be known at all.

The 127th's Surgeon is very critical of how soldiers were repeatedly diagnosed with combat fatigue rather than psychoneurosis.[24] A "victim" of combat fatigue got a brief rest, maybe even a sedative, and then returned to duty. They usually came right back, never to again be an effective soldier. Higher commands complicated the situation with their reluctance to designate soldiers as psychological cases. The Surgeon noted:

> ... the diagnosis of combat fatigue, instead of psychoneurosis, was attached in accordance with directives from higher echelons cautioning against the use of the diagnosis of psychoneurosis in combat and thus fix in the patient's mind that he was "psycho" or mentally ill. The connotation of "fatigue" and "exhaustion" denotes in the mind of the patient that quiet and rest lead to complete recovery.[25]

5,000 non-battle casualties made far worse by deliberate misdiagnosis. All those replacements, 6,000 of them, were not ready for war in the jungle. They were mostly green kids, 18-20 years old, and many would wind up in the hospital. They could not even lean on veterans due to their own rampant exhaustion.[26] They secured a few miles of the Villa Verde Trail. Did it impact anything? Not really.

"It's pretty hard to tell you know after all these years, just how I felt during the battle on the Villa Verde Trail in Luzon, beginning in January and lasting until the end of the summer. But it was a fact that the 32nd Division was given a mission that was too big for its ability. No question in my mind."[27] So stated General Gill, and he was absolutely right. The Villa Verde Trail with its formidable defensive advantages and tenacious enemy was too much for a single, understrength division. They did persevere, but at great cost. Fortunately, the atomic bomb made any further action on their part unnecessary.

Bibliography

Canon, M. Hamlin. *Leyte: The Return to The Philippines.* Washington D.C.: Center of Military History, 1954.

Carlisle, John M. *Red Arrow Men: Stories About the 32nd Division on the Villa Verde Trail.* Nashville: The Battery Press, 1990.

I Corps. I Corps: History of the Luzon Campaign, Philippine Islands, 1945. Headquarters: I Corps, 1945.

Sixth United States Army. *Report of the Luzon Campaign: 9 January – 30 June 1945*. Headquarters: Sixth United States Army, 1945.

Smith, Edward Jaquelin. *Always A Commander: The Reminiscences of Major General William Gill*. Colorado Springs: The Colorado College, 1974.

Smith, Robert Ross. *The Approach to The Philippines*. Washington D.C.: Office of The Chief of Military History, 1974.

——.*Triumph in The Philippines*. Washington D.C.: Center of Military History, 1963.

Young, Robert. *Pacific Hurtgen: The American Army in Northern Luzon, 1945*. Washington D.C: Westphalia Press, 2017.

32nd Infantry Division. *After Action Report: Mike I Operation, Luzon, January 27 – June 30, 1945*. Headquarters: 32nd Infantry Division, 1945.

127th Infantry Regiment. *History of the 127th Infantry Regiment – Luzon Campaign: 27 January 1945 – 30 June 1945*. Headquarters: 127th Infantry Regiment, 32nd Infantry Division, 1945.

127th Infantry Regiment. *Surgeon's Report: Luzon Campaign*. Headquarters: 127th Infantry Regiment, 32nd Infantry Division, 1945.

Notes

1 Cannon, M. Hamlin, *Leyte: The Return To The Philippines*, 220-227.

2 Ibid., 368.

3 Robert Ross Smith, *The Approach To The Philippines*, 505.

4 John Carlisle, *Red Arrow Men: Stories About the 32nd Division on the villa Verde Trail*, 7.

5 To best understand this debate see the memoirs of General MacArthur and his staff as well as Admiral Chester Nimitz and his staff officers. All have to be taken very carefully as there is blatant bias in each account and each defense of their strategic point of view.

6 Sixth United States Army, *Report of the Luzon Campaign: 9 January – 30 June 1945*, 80.

7 The 32nd "Red Arrow" Veterans Association, *The 32nd Infantry Division in World War II, The "Red Arrow" Luzon Campaign – The Villa Verde Trail*, 2.

8 Smith, *Triumph In The Philippines*, 504.

9 Edward Jaquelin Smith, *Always A Commander: The Reminiscences of Major General William Gill*, 84.

10 I Corps, *I Corps: History Of The Luzon Campaign, Philippine Islands, 1945*, 63.

11 32nd-division.org

12 Smith, *Triumph In The Philippines.* 409

13 Robert Young, *Pacific Hurtgen*, 99-101.

14 32nd Infantry Division, After Action Report, 23-4

15 127th Infantry Regiment, *Surgeon's Report: Luzon Campaign*, 8.

16 Young, 104-5.

17 Edward Jaquelin Smith, *Always A Commander: The Reminiscences of Major General William Gill*, 87.

18 Ibid.

19 Statistics on replacements and programs to integrate them as well as the condition of men returning from hospitals are taken from the 32nd Infantry Division After Action Report, Annex #1, G-1 Report, 1-3.

20 Robert B. Vance, Lt. Colonel, *Action On Hill 505*, 2.

21 127th Infantry Regiment, *History of the 127th Infantry Regiment – Luzon Campaign*, 5.

22 Young, 110-111.

23 32nd Infantry Division, *After Action Report, Annex #1, G-1 Report*, 1.

24 127th Infantry Regiment, *Surgeon's Report: Luzon Campaign*, 9.

25 Ibid.

26 Ibid., 9.

27 Edward Jaquelin Smith, *Always A Commander: The Reminiscences of Major General William Gill*, 87.

The Jewishness of the Babatha Archive

Mary Jo Davies
American Public University

Abstract

In the 1960s, in a cave at Nahal Hever near the western bank of the Dead Sea, archaeologist Yigael Yadin discovered the bones of many bodies belonging to men, women, and children, along with copious amounts of papyri stowed away in a crevice of the cave. This discovery dates back to the second-century AD. This study will examine the significance of one of the archives that belonged to a woman named Babatha and which provides a rich array of evidence regarding the life of Jewish women under Roman rule in second-century Arabia Petraea. More significantly it will reveal that Jews living in this Roman occupied region were not as romanized as some historians claim.

Keywords: Hellenization, Mishnah, Pentateuch, Aramaic, Justinian, Arabia Petraea, Nabatean, Ketubbah, Rabbinic

El judaísmo de los archivos de Babatha

Resumen

En la década de 1960, en una cueva de Nahal Hever cerca de la orilla occidental del Mar Muerto, el arqueólogo Yigael Yadin descubrió los huesos de muchos cuerpos pertenecientes a hombres, mujeres y niños, junto con copiosas cantidades de papiros guardados en una grieta de la cueva. Este descubrimiento se remonta al siglo II d.C. Este estudio examinará la importancia de uno de los archivos que perteneció a una mujer llamada Babatha y que proporciona una rica variedad de pruebas sobre la vida de las mujeres judías bajo el dominio romano en la Arabia Petraea del siglo II. Más significativamente, revelará que los judíos que vivían en esta región ocupada por los romanos no estaban tan romanizados como afirman algunos historiadores.

Palabras clave: Helenización, Mishná, Pentateuco, Arameo, Justiniano, Arabia Petraea, Nabateo, Ketubbah, Rabínico

Babatha档案的犹太性

摘要

20世纪60年代，在死海西岸附近的纳哈尔赫维尔河谷（Nahal Hever）的一个洞穴中，考古学家Yigael Yadin发现了许多男性、女性和儿童的尸骨，还在洞穴的一条缝隙中发现了大量的莎草纸。该发现追溯到公元二世纪。本研究将分析其中一个档案的重要性，这份档案属于一个名叫Babatha的女人，它提供了丰富的证据，关于公元二世纪阿拉伯佩特拉地区的犹太女人在古罗马统治下的生活。更重要的是，本研究将揭示在该古罗马占领地区中生活的犹太人并不像一些历史学家认为的那么罗马化。

关键词：希腊化，《密西拿》，《摩西五书》，阿拉姆语，查士丁尼，阿拉伯佩特拉，纳巴泰人，婚书，拉比

The Bar Kokhba Revolt of 132 CE was the final in a series of Jewish rebellions against Roman occupation. When Hadrian first became the Roman emperor in 118 CE, he initially allowed the Jews to return to Jerusalem to rebuild the Holy Temple, which the Romans had destroyed in 70 CE following the failure of the first Jewish revolt (66–73 CE). However, Hadrian quickly retracted his word. By 123 CE, the Jews began to launch surprise guerilla attacks against the Romans. Roughly nine years later they began an organized rebellion under the guidance of Jewish military leader Simon Bar-Kokhba, who had previously succeeded in expelling Roman officials stationed in En-Gedi, a fertile desert oasis located within the boundaries of Arabia Petraea on the western banks of the Dead Sea near Masada and the Qumran caves. Simon Bar-Kokhba exerted unlimited authority over his army of 400,000 soldiers. In 132 CE, he led them on this final revolt against the Romans, which lasted three years.[1] Hadrian had pushed the Jews to the limit when he established the city of Aelia Capitolina on the ruins of Jerusalem and began to build a temple to Jupiter on the site of the destroyed Holy Temple.[2]

Historian Werner Eck echoed second century historian Cassius Dio when he stated that the war was widespread, extending from Judaea to Arabia, and even into Syria.[3] In *Roman History*, Dio said, "all Judaea had been stirred up, and the Jews everywhere were gathering together, and giving evidence of great hostility to the Romans, partly by secret and partly by overt acts; many outside nations, too, were joining them through eagerness for gain, and the whole earth, one might almost say, was being stirred up over the matter."[4]

Figure 1. Cave of Letters where Babatha's archive was found.
Israel Antiquities Authority. Licensed under Creative Commons.

Figure 2. Obverse and reverse of the first coin issued in Judaea, Aelia Capitolina.
Struck 136 CE. Classical Numismatic Group, Inc. Licensed under Creative Commons.

the pieces of their lives. But that was not to be. Presumably, the Romans discovered their hiding place and forced them to either surrender to provincial authorities, or to stay there and die of starvation. Many surrendered and were sold into slavery; some were transported to Egypt.[5] Simon Bar-Kokhba eventually died in a massive battle in the year 135 CE.

Nearly two thousand years later, in the 1960s, in a cave at Nahal Hever, archaeologist Yigael Yadin discovered the bones of many bodies belonging to men, women, and children, along with copious amounts of papyri stowed away in a crevice of the cave. This study examines the significance of an archive of legal documents found in the cave that belonged to a woman named Babatha.

While papyrological evidence supports the fact that she had been in the cave, there is no record of whether she surrendered to the Romans or whether some of the bones found in the cave belonged to her. Nevertheless, Babatha's archive provides a rich array of evidence regarding the life of Jewish women under Roman rule in second-century Arabia Petraea. More significantly, this study reveals that Jews living in this Roman occupied region were not as romanized as some historians claim.

Figure 3. A scroll found in the cave; part of the Babatha archive. Second century CE. Licensing: this work is in the public domain in its country of origin.

As the Roman soldiers marched along the western shore of the Dead Sea toward the Jewish stronghold stationed in En-Gedi, many of the inhabitants fled to the Judaean desert and hid in the desert caves. Along with valuable and necessary daily items, some of the inhabitants also brought with them numerous important legal documents that affirmed legal rights to their possessions. They hoped to remain in the caves only until the end of the rebellion and then return home to pick up

The documents of the desert caves demonstrate that legal practitioners and scribes drafted most legal papers in Greek, which was the official language of Roman legal administration in the provinces. Although the Romans had introduced their legal system in the region, they left local customs, such as marriage and law of succession, to indigenous traditions. However, at this time, Jewish rabbis had not yet completed the *Mishnah*—a book of Jewish laws written by scholars throughout the second century and codified at the beginning of the third.

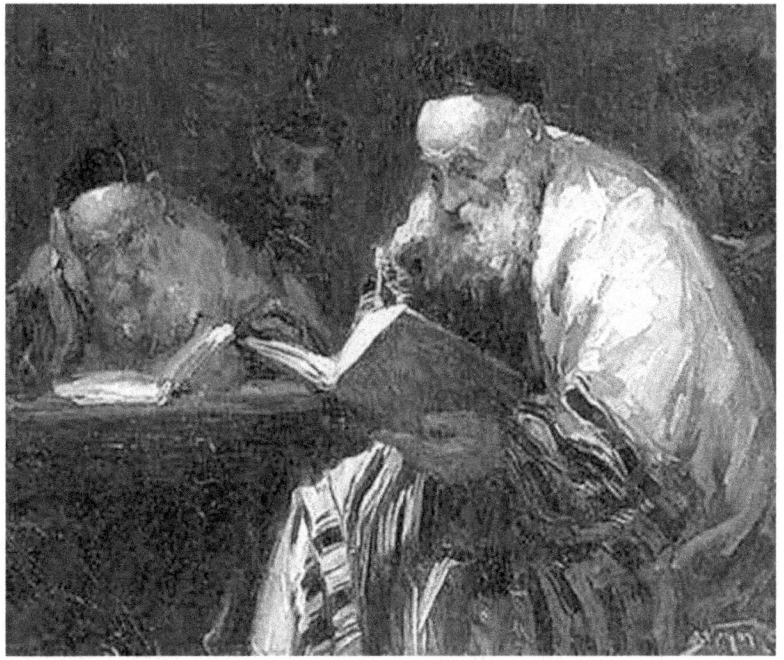

Figure 4. Talmud Readers by Adolf Behrman (1876–1942). Licensing: this media file is in the public domain in the United States.[6]

Because of this, there is a trend in Jewish historical study of the second century CE to claim that rabbinic influence had no significant impact on the lives of Jews. This claim relies, in part, on the assumption that by this time the Roman legal system had influenced most Jews, and that this was the reason they wrote their documents in Greek. However, this claim fails to consider that the Romans may have not been familiar with the local indigenous dialects of their provinces. They were, however, very familiar with the Greek language since they had annexed Greece centuries earlier. Some Roman provinces, such as Egypt, were also familiar with the Greek language, since Alexander the Great (356–323 BCE) had conquered it in the fourth century BCE. Professor of Calvary Baptist Theological Seminary Larry R. Thornton stated that Alexander's founding of cities, minting of money, training of soldiers, encouraging intermarriage, and funding Greek arts and sciences all contributed to the enduring Hellenization of the regions he conquered.[7] This is likely the reason why the Romans chose to use a language their provinces understood: Greek. However, knowledge of the Greek language was not as ingrained in Arabia Petraea the way it was among the peoples of other Roman provinces. While Alexander had conquered Arabia around 324 BCE, he had left that region autonomous; hence, the Greek conquest of Arabia never lead to the Hellenization of that region. Nevertheless, since Greek was the most commonly understood language throughout the other Roman provinces, it became the language of choice for Roman legal administration in Arabia Petraea as well.

Historian Jacobine G. Oudshoorn further stated that a legal practitioner's choice of language and legal forms was not necessarily related to the court or legal system that the provincials used.[8] Some documents written in Greek, on Greek forms and presented in the Roman courts, clearly reflected Jewish customs. Some also reflected Roman and Jewish influences in a single papyrus. In other words, the choice to draft legal documents in the Greek language for the Roman courts should not automatically imply that the provincial population of Arabia Petraea had abandoned their own legal traditions in favor of Roman ones.

A close inspection of some of Babatha's legal affairs reveals the way people sometimes used Jewish customs and Roman laws on opposing sides of a single case. *P. Yadin* 21, *P. Yadin* 23, and *P. Yadin* 25 prove this claim.[9] *P. Yadin* 21 was a contract that Babatha had drawn up to settle her late husband's debt—money he owed to her—by temporarily seizing his date orchards and collecting the money from the sale of the crop. However, the orchards now legally belonged to her late husband's sons from a previous marriage. Apparently, they did not repay Babatha what their late father owed to her. By temporarily seizing the orchards, Babatha was acting in accordance with an old Jewish custom of self-help, which sometimes allowed Jews to circumvent the court system to settle a dispute. *P. Yadin* 23 was a summons that her late husband's sons served to Babatha, which stated the illegality of her action, but it was based on a Roman law that considered her appropriation of the orchards a violent act. With clear Jewish legal tradition in mind, in *P. Yadin* 25, Babatha rejected her stepson's summons, calling it a "false charge."[10]

Prior to the Bar Kokhba revolt, Jews in Arabia Petraea appeared to interact in a relatively diplomatic fashion with their new rulers. Roman authorities had not prohibited them from using their age-old oral laws. The oral laws were a legal interpretation of the first five books of the Torah known as the Pentateuch. These books (Genesis, Exodus, Leviticus, Numbers, and Deuteronomy) are collectively known as the *Law*.

While the authors of the Mishnah would not complete their written book of laws until the early third century CE, Jews did continue to live by their age-old Jewish mores.

During the early years of the Roman occupation of Arabia Petraea (106 CE), legal practitioners initially continued to follow Jewish tradition by writing legal documents in Aramaic and Nabatean on local juridical forms. Historian Kimberley Csajkowski attributed this to several different reasons, one of which assumed that since access to reliable Greek scribes may not have initially been commonplace, Jews continued to rely on their own local scribes.[11] Nevertheless, historian Adi Wasserstein observed that rabbinic customs did not oppose the use of non-Jewish legal forms or procedures and perhaps even arranged for incorporating its own rules with non-Jewish ones.[12]

At some point between 122 and 124 CE, however, Jewish litigants began to draft many of their legal documents in Greek, on Greek legal forms, but this did not necessarily mean that the Jewish people had abandoned their own legal traditions. While none of Babatha's documents contain the kind of religious language typically stressed in the divine Jewish commandments, it is clear that some of the documents do explicitly reflect the use of Jewish legal customs. This calls into question historian Hannah M. Cotton's strong affirmation that the "Jewishness" of the desert archives is expressed only in the Aramaic signatures.[13] Both Cotton and historian Ze'ev Safrai have also suggested that Greek was used to enforce the validity of the legal documents in a Greek-speaking court.[14] Historian Tiziana J. Chiusi similarly stated that Babatha might have felt that Roman legal instruments would be more effective in achieving her goals.[15]

Oudshoorn questioned some of these conclusions because they never really attempted to address the larger issue: that perhaps Roman and local laws might have been co-equal legal systems and that both systems might have even

Figure 5. Presentation of The Torah, by Édouard Moyse, 1860. Museum of Jewish Art and History. Licensed under Creative Commons.

been used contemporaneously.[16] However, although the Jews began to make use of Roman laws, the rabbis did urge them not to totally abandon their own legal traditions, especially since the Romans allowed Jews the freedom to use their own laws. *P. Yadin* 21—a contract regarding the sale of dates—seems to represent a strategy that was acceptable in Jewish tradition (even for Jewish widows like Babatha). Jewish people were able to legitimately circumvent the legal system by taking matters into their own hands. Because of this, historian Ranon Katsoff stated that scholars should not make blanket statements that the society reflected in the Judaean Desert documents was devoid of rabbinic authority.[17] Jewish people at this time were still clearly using rabbinic laws and traditions even when their documents were written in the Greek language, on Greek forms, and perhaps even for the Roman courts. The date orchards mentioned in *P. Yadin* 21 belonged to Babatha's late husband, Judah, son of Eleazar Khthousion. Babatha did not have any legal rights to hire permanent laborers through a labor contract. That right belonged to her late husband's heirs (adult sons from a previous marriage). But Judah died owing Babatha money. Because of this, Babatha temporarily seized the orchards by way of a sale contract. Her intent was to sell the seasonal crop for financial restitution of her husband's debt.[18] In *P. Yadin* 21, the buyer confirms his purchase from Babatha: "I acknowledge that I have bought from you the date crop of the orchards of Judah son of Khthousion, your late husband, in Maoza called Pherora orchard and Nikarkos orchard and the third called Molkhaios's, which properties you distrain, as you say, in lieu of your dowry and debt [owed you]."[19]

Only Jewish law allowed for what Katsoff referred to as a "dodge."[20] Neither Hellenistic nor Roman law permitted a widow to protect herself in this fashion.[21] Oudshoorn stated that Babatha based her right to self-help on her *ketubba* (dowry)—a document written in Aramaic and clearly reflecting Jewish law.[22] Babatha was acting in accordance with Jewish oral tradition that the rabbis would eventually postulate seventy years later in the Mishnah. This Mishnaic law states, "[a] widow, whether she became a widow after betrothal or after wedlock, may sell [property that was security for her *Ketubah*] without the consent of the court."[23] In Babatha's ketubba (*P. Yadin* 10) her husband, Judah, stipulated,

> if I should go to my eternal h[ome] before you, you will [re]side, and (continue to) be provided for from my "house" and from my properties, [until the t]ime that my [heir]s will agree to give you the silver of your *ketubba*. And whenever [you] tell me, [I will exchange] for [you this document, as is fitting. And all properties that I possess and that I will acquire are guaranteed and pledged.]"[24]

Judah eventually died. In her book *Chattel or Person?* historian Judith Romney Wegner stated that upon the death of a husband, a Jewish widow can immediately gain access to her dowry.[25] She could also defer this claim, in which case the rightful heirs of the deceased husband would support her. In the Mishnah, *M. Ket.* 11:1 states, "The widow receives her maintenance from the property of the orphans."[26] It is clear from Babatha's ketubba that this Mishnaic law had already been practiced long before the Mishnah was ratified. However, Babatha's problem was that while her deceased husband's heirs might have been providing for her maintenance as stipulated in her ketubba, her husband had died owing her 300 denarii of silver, which she had loaned to him so that he could provide for his daughter, Shelamzion's, marriage.[27] *P.*

Yadin 17 stated that if her husband did not promptly reimburse Babatha, he would be liable to repay her "twofold in addition to damages, and he shall also be answerable to a charge of illegality in such matters."[28] More significantly, it stated that Babatha had "the right of execution upon Judah and all his possessions everywhere—both those which he possesses and those which he may validly acquire in addition."[29]

Judah's sons and rightful heirs clearly did not repay Babatha what their late father owed to her. Perhaps they continually postponed or disregarded Babatha's requests, for whatever reason. In all likelihood, this gave rise to antagonism between Babatha and her late husband's heirs. In accordance with the Jewish custom of self-help, Babatha settled her late husband's debt by seizing the date orchards and collecting the money from the sale of the seasonal crop. Although the money her late husband owed to her was not part of the security for her ketubba, Babatha likely felt that she could use the conditions of *P. Yadin* 17 to justify her right to temporarily seize the orchards in accordance with the Jewish tradition of self-help.

This throws into question Cotton's statement: "Babatha and her litigants show no awareness of an existing normative rabbinic law, but are strongly influenced by Roman law."[30] Babatha may have been an illiterate—as archival evidence shows—but this does not necessarily mean that she was uninformed.[31] Even if she had been uninformed about the intricacies of existing rabbinic practice, people close to her may have warned her that Roman law would not have protected her and that in Jewish practice, a dodge was permissible. Her adroit use of the dodge reveals the way she (and no doubt many other Jews of her time) continued to turn to Jewish practices even while under Roman rule. The people who outlined *P. Yadin* 21 had Jewish law in mind even though they wrote the contract in Greek.[32] Babatha likely did not want to deal with all the legal wrangling by petitioning the governor to oblige her late husband's heirs to repay the debt, so she bypassed this approach by taking matters into her own hands.

Although Babatha's appropriation of these date orchards was legally permissible under Jewish custom, Judah's sons, represented by an elite Roman woman, Julia Crispina, challenged her right to do so in the court of the provincial Roman governor. In *P. Yadin* 23 Besas, one of Judah's sons and heirs, summoned Babatha to meet him before Haterius Nepos, the provincial magistrate, "in the matter of a date orchard devolving to the said orphans which you hold in your possession by force."[33] Roman law considered Babatha's forceful arrogation of her late husband's orchards a violent act.

Justinian's *Digest* represented Roman laws. When Justinian became the ruler of the Byzantine Empire in 527 CE, he ordered the compilation of three books representing Roman laws. One of these books was the *Digest*. Known also as the *Code*, a team of sixteen academic lawyers assembled it in an effort to legally bind everything of value from earlier Roman law.

haps Judah's heirs, with their representative Julia Crispina, felt that they had an edge over Babatha by forcing her to appear before the Roman governor to fight for their rights in accordance with Roman law.[36]

Historian Ann Ellis Hanson states that stressing the violent behavior of an adversary was an acceptable stylistic strategy in the legal documents of Egypt (more specifically Greco-Roman Egypt). [37] One such example can be found in *Women & Society in Greek and Roman Egypt*, edited by Jane Rowlandson, which shows the way a woman appealed to the prefect for compensation from two dishonest business managers she had hired. Using emotional language, the petition states,

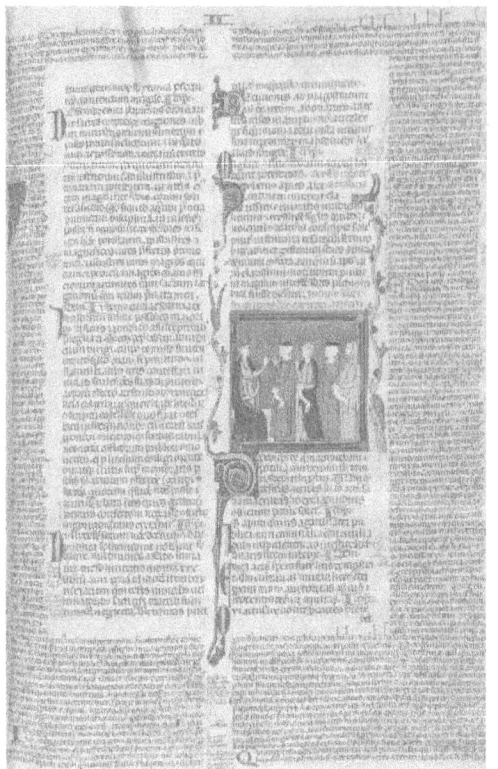

Figure 6. Excerpt from the manuscript "Codex Justiniani I-IX." Medieval copy of the famous Code of Justinian. Copied by Franciscus Accursius in the 13th century. Preserved in the Ghent University Library. Licensed under Creative Commons.

Oudshoorn stated that some of the lawyers cited in the *Digest* lived in the second century CE; hence, the legal opinions of some lawyers cited in the *Digest* date from the same period as Babatha's archive.[34] A violent act, according to the *Digest*, is not limited solely to physical injury, but includes "whenever anyone demands what he thinks is owed to him otherwise than through the agency of a judge."[35] This Roman law could apparently be (and indeed was) applied to a summons that clearly reflected Jewish law—in this case, the Jewish law of succession. Per-

[t]hese men conducted themselves dishonestly and robbed me, and depriving me of the property I placed in their hands, they never submitted to me proper accounts; and similarly, by giving way in the business they conducted, they stole from me two oxen from those which I have for [ploughing? or irrigation?] of my same estates, despising my lack of business sense.[38]

However, the use of such emphatic, accusatory language in legal documents was not customary to the Jews in Arabia Petraea even after Roman occupation. *P. Yadin* 15 provides a good example of this. Babatha had been previously married to another man by the name of Jesus. Together they had a son, also named Jesus. Upon the death of her first husband, two guardians were appointed to provide Babatha with a monetary allowance for the financial welfare of their underage son. Over time, one of the guardians fell short of his duty. In 125 CE, Babatha issued a summons—*P. Yadin* 15. In poised, official language, her summons states,

> On account of your not having given . . . to my son, the said orphan . . . just as 'Abdoobas son of Ellouthas, your colleague, has given by receipt, therefore I summon you to attend the court of the governor Julius Julianus in Petra the metropolis of Arabia until we are heard in the tribunal of Petra on the second day of the month of Dios(?) or at his next sitting in Petra.[39]

Several years later, using the same temperate tone in *P. Yadin* 25, Babatha rejected her second husband's son's emphatic claim of a violent act, calling it a "false charge."[40] Using Jewish law, which allowed Babatha to take legal matters into her own hands, Babatha counteracted a summons that was clearly based on Roman law.

For centuries, Judaism's leading rabbis had resisted writing down the oral law. They believed that verbally imparting its principles would oblige students to maintain a close relationship with their teachers, whom they believed to be the best preceptors of Jewish legal tradition. However, the various rebellions against Roman occupation cost the Jewish population throughout Arabia Petraea well over a million lives—among them thousands of rabbinical scholars. The drop in the number of Jewish scholars may have played a decisive role in Rabbi Judah the Prince's decision, in the second century CE, to set the oral law down in writing in an effort to avoid suffering the loss of their ancestral traditions.[41] While archival evidence as to the outcome of Babatha's case is lost to history, what is left to us does reveal that although the Romans had introduced their legal system in the region, the Jewish people of second-century Arabia Petraea often continued to turn to their own legal traditions to settle disputes. Despite the fact that the Mishnah would not be codified for another seventy years or so, they had not wholly abandoned their ancestral Jewish customs in favor of Roman ones.

Bibliography

Primary Sources

Cotton, Hannah M. and A. Yardeni. *Aramaic, Hebrew and Greek Documentary Texts from Nahal Hever and Other Sites, with an Appendix Containing Alleged Qumran Texts (The Seiyal Collection II), DJD XXVII*. Translated by Matthew Morgenstern. Oxford: Clarendon Press, 1997.

Dio, Cassius. *Roman History*. Translated by Ernest Cary, Ph.D. Vol. 8. New York: G.P. Putnam's Son, 1925. https://archive.org/details/L176CassiusDioCocceianusRomanHistoryVIII6170/page/n457/mode/2up.

Lewis, Naphtali, ed. *The Documents from the Bar Kokhba Period in the Cave of Letters: Greek Papyri, with Aramaic and Nabatean signatures and subscriptions*. Jerusalem: Hebrew University of Jerusalem, 1989.

Rowlandson, Jane, ed. *Women and Society in Greek and Roman Egypt: A Sourcebook*. New York: Cambridge University Press, 1998.

Danby, Herbert, trans. *The Mishnah*. Oxford: Oxford University Press, 1933. https://archive.org/details/DanbyMishnah/page/n9/mode/2up.

Watson, Alan, ed. *The Digest of Justinian*, Vol. 4. Philadelphia: University of Pennsylvania Press, 1985.

Secondary Sources

Bagnall, Roger S. *Egypt in Late Antiquity*. New Jersey: Princeton University Press, 1993.

Casajkowski, Kimberley. *Localized Law: The Babatha and Salome Komaise Archives*. Oxford: Oxford University Press, 2017.

Chroust, Anton-Hermann. "Legal Profession in Ancient Imperial Rome." *Notre Dame Law Review* 30, no. 4 (1955): 521–616. https://scholarship.law.nd.edu/cgi/viewcontent.cgi?article=3652&context=ndlr.

Cotton, Hannah M. "A Cancelled Marriage Contract from the Judaean Desert." *The Journal of Roman Studies* 84 (1994): 64–86. https://www.jstor.org/stable/300870.

———. "The Guardian (Epitropoç) of a Woman in the Documents from the Judaean Desert." *Zeitschrift Für Papyrologie Und Epigraphik* 118 (1997): 267–273.

———. "The Guardianship of Jesus son of Babatha: Roman and Local Law in the Province of Arabia." *The Journal of Roman Studies* 83 (1993): 94–108. https://www.jstor.org/stable/300980.

———. "The Rabbis and the Documents." In *Jews in a Graeco-Roman World*, ed. Martin Goodman, 167–179. New York: Oxford University Press, 1999.

Chiusi, Tiziana J. "Babatha vs. the Guardians of Her Son: A Struggle for Guardianship—Legal and Practical Aspects of P. Yadin 12-15, 27." In *Law in the Documents of the Judaean Desert*, ed. Ranon Katsoff and David M. Schaps, 105-132. Leiden Boston: Brill, 2005.

Eck, Werner. "The Bar Kokhba Revolt: The Roman Point of View." *The Journal of Roman Studies* 89 (1999): 76-89. https://www.jstor.org/stable/300735.

Hanson, Ann Ellis. "The Widow Babatha and the Poor Orphan Boy." In *Law in the Documents of the Judaean Desert*, ed. Ranon Katsoff and David M. Schaps, 85-103. Leiden Boston: Brill, 2005.

Ilan, Tal. "Premarital Cohabitation in Ancient Judea: The Evidence of the Babatha Archive and the *Mishnah*." *The Harvard Theological Review* 86 no.3 (1993): 247-264. https://www.jstor.org/stable/1510010.

Katsoff, Ranon. "'P. Yadin 21' and Rabbinic Law on Widows' Rights." *The Jewish Quarterly Review* 97 no. 4 (2007): 545-575. https://www.jstor.org/stable/25470227.

Jewish Virtual Library: A Project of AICE. "Ancient Jewish History: The Bar-Kokhba Revolt: (132-135 CE)." Accessed August 14, 2020. https://www.jewishvirtuallibrary.org/the-bar-kokhba-revolt-132-135-ce.

Jewish Virtual Library: A Project of AICE. "Judaism: The Oral Law—Talmud & Mishna." Accessed August 14, 2020. https://www.jewishvirtuallibrary.org/the-oral-law-talmud-and-mishna.

Jewish Virtual Library: A Project of AICE. "Shimon Bar Kokhba: (c. 15-135)." Accessed August 17, 2020. https://www.jewishvirtuallibrary.org/shimon-bar-kokhba.

Oudshoorn, Jacobine G. *The Relationship between Roman and Local Law in the Babatha and Salome Komaise Archives: General Analysis and Three Case Studies on the Law of Succession, Guardianship and Marriage.* Boston: Brill, 2007.

Safrai, Ze'ev. "Halakhic Observance in the Judaean Desert Documents." In *Law in the Documents of the Judaean Desert*, ed. Ranon Katsoff and David M. Schaps, 205-236. Leiden Boston: Brill, 2005.

Thornton, Larry R. "Alexander the Great and Hellenization." *Calvary Baptist Theological Journal*, Spring (1988): 25-42.

Wasserstein, Adi. "A Marriage Contract from the Province of Arabia Nova: Notes on Papyrus Yadin 18." *The Jewish Quarterly Review*, New Series 80 no.1/2 (1989): 93-130. https://www.jstor.org/stable/1454328.

Wegner, Judith Romney. *Chattel or Person? The Status of Women in the Mishnah.* New York: Oxford University Press, 1988.

Notes

1 "Shimon Bar Kokhba: (c. 15-135)," Jewish Virtual Library: A Project of AICE, accessed August 17, 2020, https://www.jewishvirtuallibrary.org/shimon-bar-kokhba.

2 "Ancient Jewish History: The Bar-Kokhba Revolt: (132-135 CE)," Jewish Virtual Library: A Project of AICE, accessed August 14, 2020, https://www.jewishvirtuallibrary.org/the-bar-kokhba-revolt-132-135-ce.

3 Werner Eck, "The Bar Kokhba Revolt: The Roman Point of View," *The Journal of Roman Studies* 89 (1999): 78, https://www.jstor.org/stable/300735.

4 Cassius Dio, *Roman History* VIII 69.13.1-2; translation by Ernest Cary, PhD (New York: G.P. Putnam's Son, 1925), Archive.org.

5 "Ancient Jewish History: The Bar-Kokhba Revolt."

6 The Talmud is a set of two books: the Mishnah, an authoritative postbiblical collection of Jewish oral laws and the *Gemara*, a rabbinic commentary on—and interpretation of—the Mishna.

7 Larry R. Thornton, "Alexander the Great and Hellenization," *Calvary Baptist Theological Journal* (1988): 36.

8 Jacobine G. Oudshoorn, *The Relationship between Roman and Local Law in the Babatha and Salome Komaise Archives: General Analysis and Three Case Studies on the Law of Succession, Guardianship and Marriage* (Boston: Brill, 2007), 36.

9 Babatha's archive was published in a 1989 volume and dedicated to the memory of Yigael Yadin, the archaeologist who discovered the documents. In order to distinguish the various papyri and in honor of Yadin, the documents are numbered and referred to as *P. Yadin.* The letter "P" refers to "papyri."

10 *P. Yadin* 25.

11 Kimberley Casajkowski, *Localized Law: The Babatha and Salome Komaise Archives* (United Kingdom: Oxford University Press, 2017), 111.

12 Adi Wasserstein, "A Marriage Contract from the Province of Arabia Nova: Notes on Papyrus Yadin 18," *The Jewish Quarterly Review, New Series* 80:1/2 (1989): 123, https://www.jstor.org/stable/1454328.

13 Hannah M. Cotton, "A Cancelled Marriage Contract from the Judaean Desert," *The Journal of Roman Studies* 84 (1994): 64, https://www.jstor.org/stable/300870.

14 Hannah M. Cotton, "The Rabbis in the Documents," in *Jews in a Graeco-Roman World,*

ed. Martin Goodman (New York: Oxford University Press, 1999), 169; Ze'ev Safrai, "Halakhic Observance in the Judaean Desert Document," in *Law in the Documents of the Judaean Desert Documents*, edited by Ranon Katsoff and David Schaps (Boston: Brill, 2005), 225.

15 Tiziana J. Chiusi, "Babatha vs. the Guardians of her Son: a Struggle for Guardianship—Legal and Practical Aspects of P.Yadin 12–15, 27," in *Law in the Documents of the Judaean Desert Documents*, edited by Ranon Katsoff and David Schaps (Boston: Brill, 2005), 131.

16 Oudshoorn, *Relationship*, 34-36.

17 Ranon Katsoff, "'P. Yadin 21 and Rabbinic Law on Widows' Rights," *The Jewish Quarterly Review* 97: 4 (2007): 568, https://www.jstor.org/stable/25470227.

18 Ibid., 566.

19 *P. Yadin* 21.

20 Katsoff, "*P. Yadin*," 566.

21 Ibid.

22 Oudshoorn, *Relationship*, 77.

23 *The Mishnah, M. Ket.* 11.2; translation by Herbert Danby D. D. (United Kingdom: Oxford University Press, 1933), 260. Archive.org., https://archive.org/details/DanbyMishnah/page/n9/mode/2up.

24 *P. Yadin* 10.

25 Judith Romney Wegner, *Chattel or Person? The Status of Women in the Mishnah* (New York: Oxford University Press, 1988), 139.

26 *M. Ket.* 11:1.

27 Shelamzion was the sister of Judah's sons and heirs—all were Judah's children from a previous marriage.

28 *P. Yadin* 17.

29 Ibid.

30 Cotton, "A Cancelled Marriage Contract from the Judaean Desert," 64-65.

31 *P. Yadin* 15, written in the Greek language, states that Babatha needed a guardian to write for her "because of her being an illiterate."

32 Katsoff, "P. Yadin," 568.

33 *P. Yadin* 23.

34 Oudshoorn, *Relationship*, 51.

35 *The Digest of Justinian D.* 48.7.7; trans. Tony Honoré and Olivia Robinson, vol. 4, English-language trans. ed. Alan Watson (Philadelphia: University of Pennsylvania Press, 1985), 370.

36 For further reading on Julia Crispina refer to, Ilan, Tal. "Julia Crispina, Daughter of Berenicianus, a Herodian Princess in the Babatha Archive: A Case Study in Historical Identification." *The Jewish Quarterly Review* 82, no. 3/4 (1992): 361-81. https://www.jstor.org/stable/1454863.

37 Ann Ellis Hanson, "The Widow Babatha and the Poor Orphan Boy," in *Law in the Documents of the Judaean Desert,* eds. Ranon Katsoff and David M. Schaps (Leiden Boston: Brill, 2005), 102.

38 Oxyrhynchus Papyri 171 col. lines 1-16 in *Women & Society in Greek and Roman Egypt*, ed. Jane Rowlandson (New York: Cambridge University Press), 239-240.

39 *P. Yadin* 15.

40 *P. Yadin* 25.

41 "Judaism: The Oral Law—Talmud & Mishna," Jewish Virtual Library: A Project of AICE, accessed August 14, 2020, https://www.jewishvirtuallibrary.org/the-oral-law-talmud-and-mishna.

Wild West Shows: An Unlikely Vehicle for the Survival of Native American Culture in the Late Nineteenth Century

Melissa Sims
American Military University

Abstract

This essay discusses how Wild West shows, such as Buffalo Bill's Wild West Show, were places where Native Americans could safely practice their cultural and spiritual customs and traditions in the late nineteenth century. When the Bureau of Indian Affairs forced Native Americans to abandon their entire cultural system for an American one, Native Americans, like the Lakota Sioux, actively sought to participate in Wild West shows, despite being portrayed as savages and as the enemy of white settlers.

Keywords: Wild West shows, Buffalo Bill, Native Americans, Lakota Sioux, Bureau of Indian Affairs, assimilation, detribalization, reservations

Espectáculos del salvaje oeste: un vehículo poco probable para la supervivencia de la cultura nativa americana a finales del siglo XIX

Resumen

Este ensayo analiza cómo los espectáculos del salvaje oeste, como el espectáculo del salvaje oeste de Buffalo Bill, eran lugares donde los nativos americanos podían practicar con seguridad sus costumbres y tradiciones culturales y espirituales a finales del siglo XIX. Cuando la Oficina de Asuntos Indígenas obligó a los nativos americanos a abandonar todo su sistema cultural por uno estadounidense, los nativos americanos, como los Lakota Sioux, buscaron activamente participar en espectáculos del Lejano Oeste, a pesar de ser retratados como salvajes y enemigos de los colonos blancos.

Palabras clave: Espectáculos del Lejano Oeste, Buffalo Bill, Nativos Americanos, Lakota Sioux, Oficina de Asuntos Indígenas, asimilación, destribalización, reservas

狂野西部秀：19世纪末期一个不太可能让本土美国文化存活的工具

摘要

本文探讨了美国西部秀—例如布法罗·比尔的狂野西部秀—如何曾是19世纪末本土美国人安全发扬其文化和精神习俗及传统的场所。当印第安事务局强制本土美国人抛弃其全部的文化系统并遵循美国文化系统时，本土美国人—例如Lakota Sioux—试图积极参与狂野西部秀，尽管他们被描绘为野蛮人和白人殖民者的敌人。

关键词：狂野西部秀（Wild West shows），布法罗·比尔，本土美国人，Lakota Sioux，印第安事务局，同化，去部落化（detribalization），保留地

Wild West shows were among the most successful and popular forms of entertainment across the United States and Europe in the late nineteenth century. Audiences sat spellbound through hours of historical reenactments involving soldiers, cowboys, and Native Americans. It was the Indian shows, however, that made the Wild West shows so popular. Drawn from the reservations on which they lived and forced to assimilate into the white society, Native Americans were portrayed in the shows as foe, not friend of white settlers. They were meant to play the "savage" to show that there was, indeed, a need to remove them onto small, isolated reservations so that they would not hinder national expansion in the West. Despite the stereotypical portrayal of Natives as savages and the enemy of white settlers in the American West, Native Americans actively sought employment in Wild West shows. Native Americans willingly participated in the Wild West shows, like Buffalo Bill's Wild West Show, because it was the only vehicle through which they could continue practicing their cultural customs, spiritual beliefs, and language, which were being eradicated by the United States government through assimilations methods such as farming and education in Indian boarding schools.

The Indian reservation system resulted from the Federal Government's laws beginning in 1830, which eventually forced all Native American tribes into small, isolated areas west of the Mississippi River. These areas included most of present-day Oklahoma, Kansas, Colorado, New Mexico, Arizona, Wyoming, and Montana, so that white settlers could use their land for homestead building. By 1868, after a series of conflicts opposing the reservation system, known as the Indian Wars, President Ulysses S. Grant determined that the best way to end the ongoing conflicts was to assimilate the Native "savages" into mainstream society as a civilized people.

One of the first assimilation initiatives taught Native Americans how to farm, which promoted self-sufficiency. They learned animal husbandry, how and when to plant seeds, and how to use and repair tools and equipment. However, the land allotted on the reservations west of the Mississippi River, such as in the Great Plains and Northwest Territories, had short agricultural seasons or a lack of water, making the land more suitable to ranching than farming. For the few allotments suitable to farming, Indians were too poor to afford the livestock needed to plow or to purchase the necessary tools. As a result of those conditions, farming on the reservations proved to be a failure. More importantly, however, Indians were resistant to this American way of life because it "ran counter to hunter-warrior traditions."[1] Therefore, Native Americans, although resigned to life on the reservation after the collapse of armed resistance by 1890, tried to fight back and hold onto their traditional way of life.

Added to the resistance of assimilation was the continued encroachment of white settlers onto Indian lands, despite being allotted acreage through the General Allotment Act of 1887. In the end, the Act was a failure to Native Americans because it divided the reservations into smaller and smaller allotments, significantly reducing Native-owned land and making it impossible to farm the allotted land given to them and to live. Christine Haug posits that Native Americans were also cheated out of their allotments or forced to sell their land to pay their bills and have money to feed their families, adding to their growing resentment of the American way of life.[2]

Another method of the United States government to assimilate Indians into white society had to do with education. When Indian reservations were first established, missionaries set up schools to teach the English language, Protestantism, and the American way of life. By 1877, it was observed that on-reservation schools were inhibiting full American acculturation, especially in children, because they remained geographically close to their parents, who were still living according to their native customs and beliefs and speaking their native language at home. Therefore, the United States government built off-reservation boarding schools, and forced Native children as young as five years old to live away from their parents for several years to obtain an American education.

As Indian boarding schools became the leading instrument of assimilation, school officials stripped Native American youth of their cultural identity upon entering the off-reservation schools. One such school was the Carlisle Indian School in Pennsylvania, established by Richard Pratt in 1879. Pratt's goal was to "kill the Indian, and save the man."[3] The schools forced Native American children to

The Carlisle Indian School became the model for over two dozen Indian boarding schools across the United States. By 1918, the Carlisle school saw over 10,000 Native American children come through its doors. Posed on the school grounds is presumed to be 375 students, which made up the entire student body, c. 1884. Courtesy Cumberland County Historical Society.

Stripped of his Sioux culture, his long hair cut short, and dressed in American-style clothing, Luther Standing Bear stares stoically at the camera at the Carlisle Indian School, c. 1890. Courtesy National Archives and Records Administration.

pick Anglo-American names, receive Anglo-American haircuts and clothes, and speak only English. Severe punishments were administered, such as whippings and starvation, if they did not speak English. Basic subjects, such as U.S. history, and Christianity, such as the Beatitudes, were taught during one-half of the day. The second half of the day was committed to gaining knowledge in carpentry and farming for boys, and the domestic arts, like cooking and sewing, for girls.

Moreover, the off-reservation schools were hundreds of miles away from the reservations, and their conditions were so horrendous that often parents refused to send their children away; some children even ran away once from school, but Congress passed a law in 1893 that made it mandatory for Native American youth to be sent to the boarding schools. The Bureau of Indian Affairs (BIA), a federal agency that used agents assigned to each reservation to oversee that acculturation was being implemented, were authorized to send children away to school by any means necessary, including seizing children from their parents, withholding food rations from families, and jailing parents. Besides forcing the children to go to the off-reservation boarding schools, BIA agents made reservation life and assimilation difficult for Native Americans.

The Bureau of Indian Affairs was established in 1824 by Secretary of War John C. Calhoun. Its first role was to negotiate treaties between the Native tribes and the Federal Government, so that white settlers moving to the West could build their homesteads without fear of armed retaliation. According to Edmund J. Danzinger Jr., BIA agents carried out the federal laws pertaining to the tribes, but after making new treaties was banned in the wake of the Indian Wars in the 1870s, it "charged each federal agent, who was responsible for one or more reservations, with destroying tribal customs and beliefs, replacing them with mainstream American lifestyles and values, and encouraging Indian integration into dominant society."[4] Consequently, reservations became like open-air prisons.

To deconstruct Native tribes' political structures, spiritual beliefs, and customs, BIA agents administered tedious work, property, and money, which the agent often withheld for his own greedy purposes. BIA agents also controlled the actions of the chiefs and aggressively enforced farming, domesticity, the wearing of Anglo-American clothing and hairstyles, the speaking of only the English language, Christian values, and the education of their youth at Indian boarding schools.[5] Polygamy was also prohibited. Even joking about having more than one wife could mean prosecution.[6] Women were forced to give up beading and made to learn the domestic arts of cleaning, sewing, and preparing American-style meals. Furthermore, food and property sharing and gift-giving were discouraged, and religious ceremonies and dances, such as the Sun Dance, were banned because they were deemed barbaric or a form of self-torture.

A typical performance in Wild West shows involved heroic cowboys coming to the aid of a homesteading family's burning covered wagon, set on fire by the Native enemy. Courtesy David R. Phillips Collection at the McCracken Research Library.

Wild West shows promised spectators reenactments of historic events, such as the attack of the Deadwood Stagecoach and the Battle of Little Big Horn, at every show. Here, William Gordon Lillie, professionally known as Pawnee Bill, plays General Custer in a dramatic reenactment of Custer's Last Stand, c. 1905. Courtesy Library of Congress.

Moreover, no one was allowed to leave the reservation for any reason without BIA agent approval. Stephen Rockwell, author of *Indian Affairs and the Administrative State in the Nineteenth Century*, stated that although "the agent was to devote time to the welfare and improvement of the Indians in his charge," the discretion given to BIA agents by the government to use their own judgement in how to best carry out assimilation methods allowed for rampant corruption, fraud, and abuse on the reservations.[7] Historian Arrel M. Gibson argued that the "needless, agonizing, unthinkable suffering, and personal and group decline . . . matched, and in some cases, exceeded, the somber Trail of Tears."[8] Simon Pokagon, a Sioux Native, who wrote *An Indian on the Problems of His Race* in 1895, said "the [reservation] is a bad one for our people. It kills energy and begets idleness, the mother of vice. It certainly will prove a fatal blow to our people if long continued."[9] Comanche Chief Ten Bears echoed other tribal leaders, such as Crazy Horse, Sitting Bull, and Geronimo, when he said, "you wanted to put us upon a reservation . . . I do not want them . . . I was born upon the prairie . . . where there are no enclosures . . . I want to die there, and not within walls."[10] Therefore, when recruiters from the Wild West shows came to the reservations looking for Natives to join the shows, hundreds jumped at the opportunity to escape the dreadful reservation life.

Wild West shows, such as Buffalo Bill's Wild West Show (BBWWS), created by William F. Cody in 1883, were meant to educate American audiences on the "real" American West and justify national expansion. The shows entertained audiences with hours of horsemanship, marksmanship, frontier life, cowboys, white settlers, and most importantly, Native Americans.

The stars of the Wild West shows were the Native Americans, who were portrayed as American society perceived them to be—the savage enemies of white settlers who inhibited national expansion. Through the reenactment of historical events called vignettes, such as the Battle of Little Big Horn, Custer's Last Stand, and the attack on the Deadwood Stagecoach, or attacks on white families making their way West, the Native Americans were encouraged to "be themselves" and "savagely" attack soldiers, cowboys, and settlers. In a story from the *Washington Post* in 1885, the newspaper reported that "Indians, yelling like mad and exchanging rapid shots with the passengers . . . poured shot after shot into the driver . . . Spectators were spellbound."[11] An article published by the *Wheeling Register* only a few days later reported that fifteen Natives "wore their war costume. Their faces embellished with red and yellow paint, on their heads they wore immense feathers."[12] According to Alexander Erez Echelman, no matter what reenactment was being played out, the Natives were always the enemy and the white settlers the victims and the heroes, and although audiences sat in awe and applauded the attacks while the Native Americans "played Indian," they "openly engaged in Indian behavior and fought...."[13] Native Americans were depicted savagely, but they were happy to be employed in the shows.

Native Americans willingly participated in the shows for economic benefits, steady income, travel and adventure, and to learn about the "white" world in a non-threatening manner, but the main reason was because doing so allowed them to hold onto their cultural customs, beliefs, and language, which were being eradicated on the reservations.

Reservation agents detribalized Native Americans by discouraging and outlawing the practice of their cultural customs and beliefs. However, Native American customs, traditions, and native languages were encouraged in Wild West shows. Furthermore, families could stay together if all were employed in the show, which allowed Native Americans to stave off their children's acculturation in off-reservation boarding schools. They could also roam freely, whereas they could not leave the reservation without permission from the BIA agent. Those things greatly appealed to Native Americans, whose lives on the reservations were constantly overseen by corrupt and fraudulent BIA agents enforcing assimilation by any means necessary, which consequently made reservation life extremely difficult and demoralizing. BIA agents even tried putting a stop to the employment of Native Americans in the Wild West shows. In another *Washington Post* story in 1890, it was reported that "if any of the Indians should . . . attempt to leave their reservations for exhibition purposes, it will be regarded as open defiance of the authority of the government, and that prompt measures will be adopted to detain them."[14] However, Native Americans were so essential to Buffalo Bill's educational exhibitions that he paid several thousand dollars to the BIA to get "his" Indians.[15] That action allowed Native Americans to actively seek out employment in the shows. For instance, when Luther Standing Bear returned to the Pine Ridge reservation from a European tour with Buffalo Bill, he was "besieged on all sides from those who wanted to go out with the show."[16]

In the Wild West shows, as well after each show, Native Americans were highly encouraged to wear their traditional clothing, headdresses, wampums, belts, instruments of war, such as bows and arrows, and pursue beadwork and quillwork without punishment from BIA agents. Buffalo Bill reminisced in his autobiography that he "worked hard on the program entertainment, taking care to make it realistic in every detail,"[17] from their village, dances, chants, and depictions of each tribe, right down to their clothing. He even sent "men on journeys more than a hundred miles to get the right kind of war-bonnets."[18] It was imperative for Bill "to depict [the West] as it was."[19] Since the shows were to be realistic, the Sioux, Ogallala, Pawnee, Cheyenne, Cherokee, Arapaho, Sac and Fox, and Kiowa men and women employed in the shows were encouraged to keep their hair long and braided, to speak their native languages, to perform traditional dances and ceremonies, such as the Sun Dance and Ghost Dance, and to live in traditional tipis set up on the outskirts of the show. George

Dull Knife, who worked in the BBWWS for its entirety, recollected it "began to resemble the camps they had always lived in on the Plains" with campfires, women beading, men smoking and talking, and eating buffalo, away from the watchful eye of BIA agents.[20] An article appearing in the *New York Times* in 1901 related that "the Indian show is very little different behind the scenes from what he is before the curtain. When on the road he lives in wigwams, brought from his native heath, just like those quickly made ones in the show. He always wears the same costume he exhibits in the show and off the stage he revels in the same fantastic painting of his face and body."[21] John M. Burke, a recruiter for BBWWS, was asked by the same newspaper, "if the Indians' makeup for the show is his own."[22] He replied: "Indeed it is. No pale face could ever devise such curious, quaint, and significant arrangements of paint and cork. All that the Indians puts on his face and body means something. It tells of war, of peace, happiness, of misery. The Indians' garments are his own, too . . . Most of the Indian acts in the Wild West Show were devised by the redskins themselves. Their dances are their own absolutely."[23] When Buffalo Bill took his exhibition abroad to Europe, they were not discouraged from being themselves, and were allowed to live according to their cultural system openly and freely.

Luther Standing Bear, cast member in Buffalo Bill's Wild West Show, Manchester, England, c. 1902, in his Sioux headdress, beaded breastplate, and holding a lance. Courtesy Buffalo Bill Museum and Grave, Identification Number 71.0219.

Luther Standing Bear, a Sioux educated at the off-reservation boarding school Carlisle Indian School, joined Buffalo Bill for the tour's duration. Ryan E. Burt argued that Luther Standing Bear's reason for joining Cody's troupe was directly linked to the local conditions on the Pine Ridge and Rosebud reservations, conditions closely tied to the policies of the General Allotment Act of 1887.[24] Therefore, Standing Bear jumped at the chance when Buffalo Bill asked him to join him overseas.

Luther Standing Bear wrote in his 1928 autobiography that "we were supposed to represent four different tribes," but received "no orders" on how or what to perform.[25] He continued: "each tribe was horseback," and in his performance for King Edward VII he "had a beautiful lance," and as he performed a dance in front of the king, "shook the lance in his face and danced my very prettiest," giving a few Sioux yells.[26] He concluded the recollection by saying that "when our part in the show was over we went to our village where the visitors had a chance to see how we lived."[27] This included erected tipis where they held regular council meetings and pow-wows before each show.

Standing Bear's account of his experience in BBWWS indicated that Native Americans in the Wild West shows were allowed to keep their traditional ways without persecution, while BIA agents, who believed that Wild West shows were a threat to the American acculturation of the Native American, tried to inhibit their recruitment while they forced Anglo-American lifestyles on reservation residents. The Wild West shows presented them as they were, albeit for educational purposes, but there was no glamour, everything was authentic and they were allowed to hold onto their vanishing culture and language, which is what drew them to shows like Buffalo Bill's, even if he portrayed them in a stereotypical way. Short Boy, employed in BBWWS, said he "wouldn't go back to the reservation for a new rifle and cartridges enough to last me the rest of my life."[28] That statement echoed many others, who, once their employment contracts ran out, were made to return to the reservations and don American style clothing and lifestyle again.

Although the Wild West shows, like Buffalo Bill's Wild West Show, in the late nineteenth century were more educational exhibits than entertainment shows and used to justify national expansion in the West, the shows were the only way for the Native American culture to survive at a time when the United States government believed it was best to stop fighting them and assimilate them into mainstream white society through the eradication of their entire cultural system. Forcing them off their native lands and onto small, isolated reservations where they were also forced to acculturate into American citizens through farming, education, and the replacement of their cultural identity with an American one made Native Americans actively and consciously seek out employment in Wild West shows. To them, that was the only way to avoid the attempts of the Federal Government and Bureau of Indian Affairs agents to assimilate them; there, they could hide their culture in plain sight. Although Wild West shows portrayed Native Americans as savages and the enemy of white settlers in the American West through reenactments of attacks on the battlefield or on the prairie, they willingly "played Indian" to keep their culture alive when there was no other place to do so freely and safely in the late nineteenth century.

Bibliography

Burt, Ryan E. ""Sioux Yells" in the Dawes Era: Lakota "Indian Play," the Wild West, and the Literatures of Luther Standing Bear." *American Quarterly* 62, no. 3 (2010): 617-37. http://www.jstor.org/stable/40983422.

Cody, William F. *An Autobiography of Buffalo Bill*. New York: Farrar and Rinehart Incorporated, 1920. Kindle.

"Col. Cody Get His Indians: Mr. Morgan Finds He Is Not A Bigger Man Than Mr. Noble." *New York Times*. March 4, 1891. Retrieved from http://codyarchive.org/texts/wfc.nsp01426.html. Accessed April 19, 2018.

Danzinger, Edmund J., Jr. "Native American Resistance and Accommodation during the Late Nineteenth Century." In Charles C. Calhoun (Ed.), *The Gilded Age: Perspectives on the Origins of Modern America* (pp.167-186). Lanham, MD: Rowman and Littlefield Publishers, 2007.

Echelman, Alexander Erez. "A Contested Future: Buffalo Bill's Wild West, Native American Performers, and the Military's Struggle for Control Over Indian Affairs, 1868-1898." *Senior Project 2015*. Paper 169. Retrieved from *Bard College*, http://digitalcommons.bard.edu/seniorproj_s2015/139. Accessed April 17, 2018.

Fowler, Loretta. *The Columbia Guide to American Indians of the Great Plains*. Columbia University Press, 2003. Doi: 10.7312/fowl11700-005.

Gibson, Arrel M. *American Indian*. Quoted in Charles C. Calhoun (Ed.), *The Gilded Age: Perspectives on the Origins of Modern America*. Lanham, MD: Rowman and Littlefield Publishers, 2007.

Haug, Christine. "Native American Tribes and the U.S. Government." *Victorian Magazine*. 2016. Retrieved from http://www.victoriana.com/history/nativeamericans.html. Accessed April 8, 2018.

"Indians Cannot Join Wild West Shows." *Washington Post*. October 4, 1890. Retrieved from http://codyarchive.org/texts/wfc.nsp00030.html. Accessed April 19, 2018.

"Indians in the Wild West Shows." *New York Times*. April 21, 1901. Retrieved from http://codyarchive.org/texts/wfc.nsp00018.html. Accessed April 19, 2018.

"Plenty of Wild West Enthusiasm: A Group of Howling Savages Pursue a Defenseless Stage Coach." *The Washington Post*. June 23, 1885. Retrieved from http://codyarchive.org/texts/wfc.nsp00027.html. Accessed April 19, 2018.

Pokagon, Simon. *An Indian on the Problems of His People*, Albert Shaw (Ed.), New York: The Review of Reviews, 1895. Retrieved from the *University of Virginia*, http://web.archive.org/web/20110209180038/http://etext.lib.virginia.edu/etcbin/toccer-new2?id=PokIndi.sgm&images=images/modeng&data=/texts/english/modeng/parsed&tag=public&part=2&division=div2. Accessed April 19, 2018.

Pratt, Richard. "Kill the Indian, and Save the Man." Speech, On the Education of Native Americans, George Mason University, 1892. Retrieved from http://historymatters.gmu.edu/d/4929. Accessed January 17, 2021.

Rockwell, Stephen J. *Indian Affairs and the Administrative State in the Nineteenth Century*. Cambridge, NY: Cambridge University Press, 2010.

Scarangella, Linda. "Spectacular Native Performances: From the Wild West to the Tourist Site, Nineteenth Century to the Present." Doctoral thesis (2008). ProQuest Dissertations & Theses Global. (755055902). Retrieved from https://search-proquest-com.ezproxy1.apus.edu/docview/755055902?accountid=8289. Accessed April 19, 2018.

Standing Bear, Luther. *My People, the Sioux*. Edited by E.A. Brininstool. Boston: Houghton Mifflin Company, 1928. Retrieved from https://babel.hathitrust.org/cgi/pt?id=uc1.$b306020;view=1up;seq=11.

Ten Bears. "Medicine Lodge Treaty Council." 1867. In *The Gilded Age: Perspectives on the Origins of Modern America*, edited by Charles C. Calhoun. Lanham, MD: Rowman and Littlefield Publishers, 2007.

"The Wild West Visits the War Department in War Paint." *Wheeling Register*. June 28, 1885. Retrieved from http://codyarchive.org/texts/wfc.nsp00546.html. Accessed April 19, 2018

Notes

1 Edmund J. Danzinger Jr., "Native American Resistance and Accommodation During the Late Nineteenth Century," in *The Gilded Age: Perspectives on the Origins of Modern America*, ed. Charles C. Calhoun (Lanham, MD: Rowman and Littlefield Publishers, 2007), 176.

2 Christine Haug, "Native American Tribes and the U.S. Government," *Victorian Magazine*, 2016, http://www.victoriana.com/history/nativeamericans.html, accessed April 8, 2018.

3 Richard Pratt, "Kill the Indian, and Save the Man" (speech, On the Education of Native Americans, George Mason University, 1892), http://historymatters.gmu.edu/d/4929, accessed January 17, 2021.

4 Danzinger, 172.

5 Ibid.

6 Loretta Fowler, *The Columbia Guide to American Indians of the Great Plains* (New York: Columbia University Press, 2003), 87, DOI: 10.7312/fowl11700-005.

7 Stephen J. Rockwell, *Indian Affairs and the Administrative State in the Nineteenth Century* (Cambridge, NY: Cambridge University Press, 2010), 276.

8 Arrel M. Gibson, *American Indian* (Massachusetts: D.C. Heath and Co., 1979), 443, quoted in *The Gilded Age: Perspectives on the Origins of Modern America*, ed. Charles C. Calhoun (Lanham, MD: Rowman and Littlefield Publishers, 2007), 174-175.

9 Simon Pokagon, *An Indian on the Problems of His People*, ed. Albert Shaw (New York: The Review of Reviews, 1895), retrieved from the *University of Virginia*, http://web.archive.org/web/20110209180038/http://etext.lib.virginia.edu/etcbin/toccer-new2?id=PokIndi.sgm&images=images/modeng&data=/texts/english/modeng/parsed&tag=public&part=2&division=div2, accessed April 19, 2018.

10 Ten Bears, "Medicine Lodge Treaty Council" (1867), in *The Gilded Age: Perspectives on the Origins of Modern America*, ed. Charles C. Calhoun (Lanham, MD: Rowman and Littlefield Publishers, 2007), 169.

11 "Plenty of Wild West Enthusiasm: A Group of Howling Savages Pursue a Defenseless Stage Coach," *The Washington Post*, June 23, 1885, http://codyarchive.org/texts/wfc.nsp00027.html, accessed April 19, 2018.

12 "The Wild West Visits the War Department in War Paint," *Wheeling Register*, June 28, 1885, http://codyarchive.org/texts/wfc.nsp00546.html, accessed April 19, 2018.

13 Alexander Erez Echelman, "A Contested Future: Buffalo Bill's Wild West, Native American Performers, and the Military's Struggle for Control Over Indian Affairs, 1868-1898," *Senior Project 2015*, paper 169, retrieved from Bard College, http://digitalcommons.bard.edu/senior proj_s2015/139, accessed April 17, 2018.

14 "Indians Cannot Join Wild West Shows," *Washington Post*, October 4, 1890, http://codyarchive.org/texts/wfc.nsp00030.html, accessed April 19, 2018.

15 "Col. Cody Get His Indians: Mr. Morgan Finds He Is Not A Bigger Man Than Mr. Noble," *New York Times*, March 4, 1891, http://codyarchive.org/texts/wfc.nsp01426.html, accessed April 19, 2018.

16 Luther Standing Bear, *My People, the Sioux* (Boston: Houghton Mifflin Company, 1928), ed., E.A. Brininstool, pg. 270, https://babel.hathitrust.org/cgi/pt?id=uc1.$b306020;view=1up;seq=11.

17 William F. Cody, *An Autobiography of Buffalo Bill* (New York: Farrar and Rinehart Incorporated, 1920), 143, Kindle.

18 Ibid.

19 Ibid.

20 Quoted in Linda Scarangella, "Spectacular native Performances: From the Wild West to the Tourist Site, Nineteenth Century to the Present," (Doctoral thesis), 2008, *McMaster University*, pg. 107, pdf, file:///C:/Users/Lis/Downloads/Spectacular_Native_performance.pdf, accessed April 19, 2018.

21 "Indians in the Wild West Shows," *New York Times*, April 21, 1901, http://codyarchive.org/texts/wfc.nsp00018.html, accessed April 19, 2018.

22 Ibid.

23 Ibid.

24 Ryan E. Burt, "Sioux Yells in the Dawes Era: Lakota Indian Play the Wild West and the Literatures of Luther Standing Bear," *American Quarterly* 62, no.3 (2010): 624, http://www.jstor.org/stable/40983422.

25 Luther Standing Bear, 252-253.

26 Ibid., 254, 256.

27 Ibid., 255.

28 Quoted in Scarangella, 103.

Book Review: Brian McAllister Linn's *The Philippine War: 1899–1902*

Lewis A. Taylor II
American Military University

Linn, Brian McAllister. *The Philippine War: 1899–1902*. Lawrence, KS: University Press of Kansas, 2000. 427 pp. ISBN: 978-0700612253.

The United States has been involved in many wars considered "forgotten" by historians, the one most mentioned being the Korean Conflict. However, there is one war that even fewer people are aware of, and that is the Philippine War of 1899 to 1902. Military historian Brian McAllister Linn, in T*he Philippine War: 1899–1902,* attempts to rectify this by crafting a comprehensive book on military operations in the Philippines.

Linn divides the book into two parts: "Conventional Operations, 1899," covering the conventional war centered mainly on the island of Luzon, and "The Archipelago, 1900-1902," covering the unconventional, guerrilla-style warfare that took place on many of the other islands that are part of the Philippine chain. By focusing on both theaters of the Philippine War, Linn can describe both a military analysis and the leadership and weaponry.

In the introduction to *The Philippine War: 1899–1902*, Linn states that it was impossible to "accord each area or campaign equal space," dealing only briefly with significant individuals or major campaigns" (ix). What Linn does cover quite well is the question of why we became involved in the Philippines. According to Linn, President McKinley did not have a firm handle on what was going on half-way around the world, because George Dewey (commander of the U.S. Asiatic Naval Squadron) "had cut the transoceanic cable" (3). Even today, the reason the United States became involved in the Philippines is "one of the most hotly debated subjects in the history of both nations"(3). According to Linn, it is possible that the involvement was "accidental and incremental" (5).

Linn covers both the First and Second Battles of Manila in-depth, and concludes that even though the Army of Liberation had approximately six months to prepare "for a showdown with the 8th Corps" (62), they did little to prepare their troops, set up a good defense, or develop tactics. Not only that, but they suffered from a lack of leadership and "failed to capitalize on the numerous American mistakes." The Army of Liberation also suffered from "[p]oor planning and logistics" (62).

The Battle of Manila demonstrated that the 8th Corps "was a tough, aggressive and capable force" and the Volunteers "proved themselves courageous and efficient fighters" (63). The Battle(s) of Manila was not only a victory for the American forces, but also raised questions about what would happen next. Would the Army of Liberation now move their operations inland, making it difficult for the American occupational forces to pursue them? Unfortunately, this movement to the inland area of the islands is exactly what happened.

The revolutionary forces adopted a guerrilla type of warfare, changing things from a conventional type of warfare to "a series of regional struggles" (185). Even though the revolutionaries suffered from a lack of weapons, they did have the ability to "blend into the population" and "were, to all outward appearances, friendly noncombatants going about their peacetime occupations" (190). This ability to disappear into the populace was a harbinger of what the United States would face in Vietnam in the 1960s and 1970s. As in Vietnam, the guerrillas in the Philippines had a difficult relationship with the population. This relationship, "one of their greatest strengths, was also a source of weakness" (197). If the population did not willingly supply and house the guerrillas, it would have to be done by force—something that needed to be avoided, if possible.

Discussion of the Philippine War, both conventional warfare and guerrilla warfare, still stimulates disagreement among historians. Linn asks if this was a war that the Filipinos lost or one that the United States won. It is often argued that the leaders of the revolution deserve the lion's share of the blame for the loss. However, the military was also guilty of many mistakes, mainly those of their leader, Emilio Aguinaldo, "who was unable to place national interests above personal gain" (323). American leadership, on the other hand, "was superior to that of its opponents, and far better than critics have given it credit for" (326). Linn concludes by stating that "the study of the Philippine War can offer great insight into the complexities of localized guerrilla war and indigenous resistance to foreign control" (328). Unfortunately, this is a lesson that the United States military did not learn, which became evident in American military operations in Vietnam.

The Philippine War: 1899–1902 is an excellent study of the conflict. The notes and bibliography are extensive and offer the opportunity to learn more about this "forgotten war."

Book Review: Peter Wallenstein's *Blue Laws and Black Codes: Conflicts, Courts and Change in Twentieth-Century Virginia*

Matt Brent

Rappahannock Community College

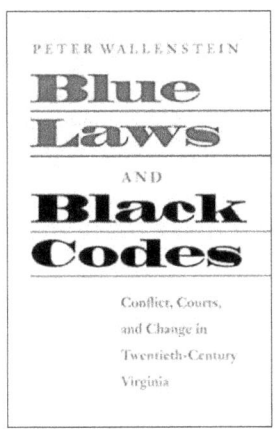

Wallenstein, Peter. *Blue Laws and Black Codes Conflict, Courts, and Change in Twentieth-Century Virginia*. Charlottesville: University of Virginia Press, 2004. 256 pp. ISBN: 978-0813922614.

Peter Wallenstein, an Associate Professor of History at Virginia Tech, has combined several of his essays about topics in Virginia history into a collection called *Blue Laws and Black Codes: Conflict, Courts and Change in Twentieth-Century Virginia*. Because of the nature of the text, each essay can be read independently of the others. Doing so, while acceptable, would severely limit one's ability to grasp Wallenstein's overall argument about the history of Virginia, the idea that traditions change because individuals sought to challenge them.

Wallenstein's collection of essays may focus on actions and events within the Commonwealth of Virginia, but it places those items in the context of both regional and national developments. Wallenstein seeks to explain that while Virginia was different from other states, it was not unique. For example, during a discussion of the construction of roads and taxes, Wallenstein demonstrates that the decision of the Supreme Court of Virginia may have differed significantly from its colleagues in the south, but it mirrored a similar decision in Nevada.

The first of Wallenstein's essays focuses on the debate over the building of roads, including how to finance them and provide the necessary labor for their construction. Titled "The Case of the Laborer from Louisa: Conscripts, Convicts and Public Roads, 1890s-1920s," it describes the court battle over the labor tax which required all able men to work two days per year on the construction of roads. To supplement the legal discussion, Wallenstein includes segments from the diary entries of individuals who describe the quality, or lack thereof, of roads in the Commonwealth. The essay demonstrates the need for change in policy as required by the needs of technology. The previously constructed roads were not sufficient to handle the newly arrived automobiles. Requiring untrained men to provide two days of labor no longer sufficed, and the various legal decisions contained in the essay explain the evolution of Virginia's road policies.

Wallenstein's second essay, "Necessity, Charity and a Sabbath: Citizens, Courts and Sunday Closing Laws, 1920s-1980s," details the gradual elimination of Blue Laws in Virginia. These legal acts prohibited various activities on Sundays. Though these laws were certainly not limited to Virginia, Wallenstein describes the legal challenges to the restrictions on Sunday activities. Once again it was the citizens who sought to challenge these prohibitions as they were seen as infringing upon the rights of individuals, and at the same time residents were less inclined to support the restrictions. Here the change demonstrates, as before, that Virginians' attitudes were evolving.

The third essay also involves legal challenges. Titled "These New and Strange Beings: Race, Sex and the Legal Profession, 1870s-1970s," this essay engages the study of changes within the field of law. Wallenstein provides a narrative that accounts for the admission of women and African-Americans to the bar in Virginia. Though not entirely focused on race, this essay provides an excellent springboard into Wallenstein's next three essays.

While the first three essays demonstrated the ability of Virginia residents to modify the constitutionality of several state laws either through constitutional amendment or through judicial actions, the following three essays primarily focus on the issue of race. Wallenstein seeks to explain the challenges to white political and social superiority within Virginia. Though the courts within Virginia had previously changed or nullified certain state laws, they upheld the various laws that purposely lessened the rights of African-Americans. Wallenstein's fourth essay describes Virginia's attempt at holding on to Jim Crow legislation that effectively segregated African-Americans on public buses and in public housing. It also chronicles the rise of influential lawyers like Oliver Hill, who would ultimately contribute to legislative changes within Virginia that would benefit African-Americans and help to bring the group towards equality.

Wallenstein continues to discuss the challenges faced by racial minorities in his next two essays. The fifth essay focuses primarily on the role of sit-ins. Using the national movement as a backdrop, he explains the significance of the events in Virginia and discusses the relevant cases that made their way through Virginia's courts. Though much of Wallenstein's fourth and fifth essays focused on the interactions of African-Americans and whites in the public eye, his sixth essay examines more private relationships. He discusses the challenges of overturning laws barring interracial marriage and chronicling the battle Mildred Jeter and Richard Loving fought in order to have their marriage legally recognized via the Supreme Court's decision in *Loving v. Virginia*.

To conclude his text, Wallenstein's final two essays focus on additional changes to the Commonwealth. The first discusses the role of redistricting within Virginia, and explains how this political act played a role in diminishing the political power of certain groups. It also focused on the period in Virginia after the prohibition of poll taxes. The final chapter targets the judicial system in Virginia, and discusses how it slowly became more diverse.

While each of the eight essays covers a different topic, Wallenstein connects them together in his discussion of the overall legal, political and societal changes taking place in Virginia in the late 19th century and throughout the 20th century. He does an effective job at presenting the concepts within the view of Virginia while at the same time extrapolating the discussion to the south as a region and the nation as a whole. His text is well documented and easy to read. It can be enjoyed by both the scholar and the casual reader.

Book Review: Lindsay M. Chervinsky's *The Cabinet: George Washington and the Creation of an American Institution*

Chris Schloemer
American Military University

Chervinsky, Lindsay M. *The Cabinet: George Washington and the Creation of an American Institution.* Cambridge: Belknap Press, 2020. 432 pp. ISBN: 9780674986480.

Lindsay M. Chervinsky, a White House historian at the White House Historical Association, has written a very readable, scholarly, and interesting book on George Washington and how he created the Cabinet as we know it. She artfully illustrates how Washington's military experiences provided lessons he brought into his presidency, how he used these lessons to manage his staff as president, and how he gradually—despite his initial reluctance—created the Cabinet.

As commander of the colonial armies, Washington used lessons learned in his experiences on British army staffs to guide him. For example, Washington observed how Lord Cornwallis treated his staff like his personal court and ruled over them, and he did not think this effective. He much preferred General Braddock's more democratic councils where all officers could have their say. He felt like Braddock treated him as part of the family and drew him into his inner circle. Washington would try to incorporate these methods with his own direct reports.

When Washington became commander-in-chief, he honed his council methods. Like Braddock, he brought his officers together in social activities. He also sent his officers written questions to answer, so he could ensure all advisors (not just the loudest) had the opportunity to share their opinions. He would then slowly consider all options privately before coming to a decision. If he felt the need, Washington would use these questions as an agenda for in-person councils. He selected talented individuals for his staff and used them wisely. The overriding purpose of these councils were to provide options, build consensus, and establish political cover for controversial decisions, such as the abandonment of New York City to the British. In that decision, his entire staff recommended the action as the position was untenable. Washington would then show this consensus to an angry Continental Congress to better defend the decision. Chervinsky observes that Washington never dictated policy, but rather preferred to gather advice and then make his own decision. Once he was elected president, however, there was no precedent for such a council.

The Constitution says nothing about a cabinet and Washington had no plans to create one. The author shows how the word "cabinet" was distasteful to many Americans, who considered King George III's cabinet a large part of the problems that ultimately resulted in revolution. In fact, although he created it, Washington never used the word "cabinet" until after he was out of office. The author shows how he also tried different alternatives, such as the Senate and Supreme Court, to act in an advisory function but found neither would work. He finally began to use his department secretaries for this purpose. After describing this process in creating the cabinet, Chervinsky gives a short biography of each of the original cabinet members.

Just as Washington selected talented army staff, he also chose experienced and knowledgeable department secretaries for his Cabinet: Henry Knox, Edmund Randolph, Thomas Jefferson, and Alexander Hamilton. The author also includes William Bradford, who after Jefferson's retirement became the second attorney general and was an instrumental part of the Cabinet. Although some have received more historical notice than others, all were good selections. Washington knew he had weaknesses and tried to select advisors who brought different skills and experience to the table. All of his appointments witnessed the Revolution as well as the struggles of the Continental Congress over the Articles of Confederation. All saw the need for a strong executive branch, but they were very conscious of how "new" everything was. Chervinsky points out time and again that Washington and his staff knew they were establishing precedents for future executive branches and were consumed with doing it right. Although Washington did not convene his first cabinet meeting until November 26, 1791 (more than two-and-a-half years into his presidency), he worked with them just as he had with his military staff.

George Washington's experiences as a military man greatly impacted his leadership style when it came to managing a staff. The author shows that he modeled his cabinet meetings after his councils of war. Once again, he sent written questions so they could provide written input, from which he could make informed decisions. Again, he used the written questionnaires to gather options, build consensus, and provide cover for controversial decisions. After a meeting, if Cabinet members did not agree, he requested written opinions to help him decide. Socially, he sought to establish camaraderie, which he had found useful as a military staff member and promoted as a commander. Washington also developed an administrative system to monitor events and correspondence, delegating details to subordinates who would represent his authority as ambassadors of the executive branch. In this way, his cabinet became indispensable to him.

The author shows how crucial the Cabinet could be, especially during times of crisis. For example, in 1793 France declared war on Great Britain and the Netherlands, and America was faced with a difficult decision. Many Americans supported the French, its first allies, but trade with Great Britain was also extremely beneficial to the American economy. In addition, America could ill afford another war with Great Britain. The Cabinet met more often that year than in any year of his presidency—upwards of five times a week. In the process, they created the first major foreign policy and adopted rules of neutrality that regulated periods of peace for decades, as Chervinsky details. They also asserted American interests in international affairs and reinforced the president's authority over diplomacy and enforcement of foreign policy, which sidelined Congress and state authorities.

And again, during the Whiskey Rebellion crisis, Washington used his cabinet for advice on shaping policy. Chervinsky portrays his actions as controversial and precedent-setting, as he asserted executive control over domestic crises while going over the heads of congressional and state authority. She shows how he used the council techniques described above before every controversial decision.

However, after most of his trusted advisors retired or resigned (described in great detail by Chervinsky), the change in personnel was difficult for Washington to adapt to. Not having the same relationship with the replacements, Washington held less meetings and sought individual advice much more often. Chervinsky also sheds light on how Washington demonstrated that the Cabinet served at his convenience, a precedent that lasts to this day.

By the time George Washington retired in 1797, he had established precedents for the presidency in its daily functions. This book describes how the Cabinet was one of his most influential creations. He made it his own private advisory body. This created flexibility for future presidents to decide how their cabinet would operate. The author describes how Adams and Jefferson followed Washington's lead in their own cabinet structure. They had different results, however, which shows how volatile such a flexible structure can be. She notes that even now, we understand how important the Cabinet is and points out that how effective a president's cabinet is depends on his ability to manage and lead it. This book is an important and original addition to the era of the founders, as well as to the understanding of a part of our government that remains influential today. It is well-written and informative. I highly recommend it.

Saber & Scroll Historical Journal

Submission Guidelines

To assist the SSHJ Editorial Staff in processing your manuscript efficiently, please follow these basic guidelines. Following these steps will ensure that our team can review your journal article promptly, and without additional work on your part. We reserve the right to reject, without further review, any submission that does not follow these guidelines or meet our high academic standards.

Thank you!
The SSHJ Editorial Staff

1. Manuscripts should be between 2,500 and 8,000 words in length, not including front or back matter, or between 800 and 1200 words for book reviews.

2. Only articles written using Microsoft Word (*.doc), and images in (*.jpeg) formats will be accepted; no *.PDF, *.TIFF or *.HEIC files.

3. The Journal's citation style is Chicago-Turabian, using end-notes, numbered in Arabic, super-script numerals, and including a complete, correctly formatted bibliography.

4. The narrative and notes are to be in 12-point Times New Roman, and the paragraphs double-spaced with a one-inch margin on all sides of the page.

5. A cover page, separate from the manuscript, must contain the following information; author's name, as they would like it to appear in print, school affiliation, if any, email address, and phone number.

6. The cover sheet must also include a statement affirming that the manuscript is not previously published material or submitted elsewhere for publication.

7. The author's name <u>should not appear</u> on the manuscript or book review to preserve the anonymity of the double-blind review process.

8. In addition to the narrative, each journal article must include a 100-150 word abstract and a list of 8-10 keywords.

9. SSHJ is always short of book reviews, so those received get immediate attention and are fast-tracked for publication.

10. We encourage authors to incorporate at least one, but no more than five, images into with their articles. Images might be photographs, paintings, illustrations, or maps

11. However, images must be of the author's creation or in the public domain. Smithsonian Open Access (https://www.si.edu/openaccess) is an excellent source.

12. A caption and source information must accompany every image. Ex: "Phineas Taylor Barnum, July 5, 1810–April 7, 1891, photographed by Matthew Brady. National Portrait Gallery NPG.97.63."

13. Our publisher prints the Journal using black text and grayscale images. Images should be approximately 300 dpi resolution.

14. SSHJ reserves the right to publish articles without any of the supplied images, substitute images that do not meet the minimum standards, or limit the number of images in an article or an issue because of space limitations.

To request additional information or submit complete articles for publication, email the Editor-in-Chief at EICSaberandScroll@apus.edu.

Featured Titles from Westphalia Press

Issues in Maritime Cyber Security Edited by Nicole K. Drumhiller, Fred S. Roberts, Joseph DiRenzo III and Fred S. Roberts

While there is literature about the maritime transportation system, and about cyber security, to date there is very little literature on this converging area. This pioneering book is beneficial to a variety of audiences looking at risk analysis, national security, cyber threats, or maritime policy.

**The Death Penalty in the Caribbean: Perspectives from the Police
Edited by Wendell C. Wallace PhD**

Two controversial topics, policing and the death penalty, are skillfully interwoven into one book in order to respond to this lacuna in the region. The book carries you through a disparate range of emotions, thoughts, frustrations, successes and views as espoused by police leaders throughout the Caribbean

**Middle East Reviews: Second Edition
Edited by Mohammed M. Aman PhD and Mary Jo Aman MLIS**

The book brings together reviews of books published on the Middle East and North Africa. It is a valuable addition to Middle East literature, and will provide an informative read for experts and non-experts on the MENA countries.

Unworkable Conservatism: Small Government, Freemarkets, and Impracticality by Max J. Skidmore

Unworkable Conservatism looks at what passes these days for "conservative" principles—small government, low taxes, minimal regulation—and demonstrates that they are not feasible under modern conditions.

**The Politics of Impeachment
Edited by Margaret Tseng**

This edited volume addresses the increased political nature of impeachment. It is meant to be a wide overview of impeachment on the federal and state level, including: the politics of bringing impeachment articles forward, the politicized impeachment proceedings, the political nature of how one conducts oneself during the proceedings and the political fallout afterwards.

Demand the Impossible: Essays in History as Activism
Edited by Nathan Wuertenberg and William Horne

Demand the Impossible asks scholars what they can do to help solve present-day crises. The twelve essays in this volume draw inspiration from present-day activists. They examine the role of history in shaping ongoing debates over monuments, racism, clean energy, health care, poverty, and the Democratic Party.

International or Local Ownership?: Security Sector Development in Post-Independent Kosovo
by Dr. Florian Qehaja

International or Local Ownership? contributes to the debate on the concept of local ownership in post-conflict settings, and discussions on international relations, peacebuilding, security and development studies.

Donald J. Trump's Presidency: International Perspectives
Edited by John Dixon and Max J. Skidmore

President Donald J. Trump's foreign policy rhetoric and actions become more understandable by reference to his personality traits, his worldview, and his view of the world. As such, his foreign policy emphasis was on American isolationism and economic nationalism.

Ongoing Issues in Georgian Policy and Public Administration
Edited by Bonnie Stabile and Nino Ghonghadze

Thriving democracy and representative government depend upon a well functioning civil service, rich civic life and economic success. Georgia has been considered a top performer among countries in South Eastern Europe seeking to establish themselves in the post-Soviet era.

Poverty in America: Urban and Rural Inequality and Deprivation in the 21st Century
Edited by Max J. Skidmore

Poverty in America too often goes unnoticed, and disregarded. This perhaps results from America's general level of prosperity along with a fairly widespread notion that conditions inevitably are better in the USA than elsewhere. Political rhetoric frequently enforces such an erroneous notion.

westphaliapress.org

Enhancing Thought Leadership and Scholarship

The Journals of American Public University System

American Public University System (APUS) proudly supports scholars worldwide through its family of peer-reviewed biannual journals:

- Space Education and Strategic Applications
- Global Security and Intelligence Studies
- International Journal of Open Educational Resources
- Journal of Online Learning Research and Practice
- Saber and Scroll Historical Journal

An innovator in online higher education, APUS—through American Military University and American Public University—excels in delivering quality affordable education to motivated working professionals.

Explore our expansive series of journals and learn why 200,000+ students and alumni have trusted APUS to help them reach their academic goals.

APUS—Celebrating 30 Years of Scholarship

Learn more at apus.edu/journals

American Public University System is accredited by the Higher Learning Commission (www.hlcommission.org) and certified to operate by SCHEV. For more about our graduation rates, the median debt of students who complete a program, and other important information, visit www.apus.edu/disclosure. 02/21

This publication is available open access at:
http://www.ipsonet.org/publications/open-access

Thanks to the generosity of the American Public University System

www.ingramcontent.com/pod-product-compliance
Lightning Source LLC
Chambersburg PA
CBHW081352040426
42450CB00016B/3413